大学英语拓展课程系列教材

U0361140

西方文化教程
AN INTRODUCTION TO
WESTERN
CULTURE

总主编 杨小彬　　主　编 陆小丽　　副主编 王　瑰

编　者（按姓氏拼音排序）

常　娟　陈虹波　卢　洁　曾靓婧
张淑芬　赵巧云　周赟赟

清华大学出版社
北　京

内 容 简 介

本书精选15个主题，内容涉及神话、建筑、绘画、教育、文学、节日、礼仪、婚俗、时尚、美食、体育、歌剧、媒体、美国大选和英国脱欧等，既让学生了解西方文化的方方面面，深入理解其文化渊源，同时提高学生的思辨能力和跨文化交际能力。每单元围绕一个话题，设计了六个板块，从单元目标、热身活动，到精读篇章、读后练习，再到学习反思与自我评价等，层层深入，将课文中所学的知识转化成能力，以培养学生的跨文化能力。

本书附配慕课资源，读者可登录https://www.xueyinonline.com/detail/207612344同步学习。

图书在版编目（CIP）数据

西方文化教程：英文 / 杨小彬主编. —北京：清华大学出版社，2018（2024.9重印）
（大学英语拓展课程系列教材）
ISBN 978-7-302-50093-3

Ⅰ.①西… Ⅱ.①杨… Ⅲ.①英语–高等学校–教材②西方文化–文化史–高等学校–教材 Ⅳ.①H319.4②K500.3

中国版本图书馆CIP数据核字（2018）第102440号

责任编辑：曹诗悦
封面设计：子 一
责任校对：王凤芝
责任印制：宋 林
出版发行：清华大学出版社
   网 址：https://www.tup.com.cn, https://www.wqxuetang.com
   地 址：北京清华大学学研大厦A座 邮 编：100084
   社 总 机：010-83470000 邮 购：010-62786544
   投稿与读者服务：010-62776969, c-service@tup.tsinghua.edu.cn
   质量反馈：010-62772015, zhiliang@tup.tsinghua.edu.cn
印 装 者：涿州市般润文化传播有限公司
经 销：全国新华书店
开 本：185mm×260mm 印 张：14.25 字 数：325千字
版 次：2018年8月第1版 印 次：2024年9月第11次印刷
定 价：62.00元

产品编号：079069-05

FOREWORD

　　党的二十大报告中明确提出"尊重世界文明多样性，以文明交流超越文明隔阂、文明互鉴超越文明冲突、文明共存超越文明优越，共同应对各种全球性挑战"的要求。我们需要加强中外文化交流、文明互鉴，推动构建人类命运共同体。《西方文化教程》一书旨在让学生了解西方文化，培养跨文化意识，拓展国际视野，在提升英语应用能力的同时提高跨文化交际能力。该教材既可作为大学生西方文化相关课程的教材，亦可作为对西方文化或提高语言技能感兴趣的学习者自学教材。

❖ 教材理念

　　"立德树人"是教育的根本任务。教育部 2020 年颁布的《大学英语教学指南》指出，大学英语课程是高等学校人文教育的一部分，兼有工具性和人文性双重性质。就人文性而言，大学英语的重要任务是进行跨文化教育，促使学生树立世界眼光，培养国际意识，提高人文素养。高校学生除了有学习、交流专业信息的需求之外，还要了解国外的社会与文化，增进对不同文化的理解，增强对中外文化异同的敏感性，树立文化自信，提高跨文化交际能力。

　　随着数智时代的到来，西方文化也正在经历着与其他文化的碰撞和融合，产生了巨大变化。我国目前的西方文化教材虽然数量较多，但有些教材存在过于学术化、难度较大、知识点较陈旧等问题，不能跟上时代的步伐；有些教材与学生的实际脱钩，导致教学目标很难实现；有些教材只有文化相关的知识介绍，忽略了学生跨文化交际能力的培养。此外，大部分教材只有纸质材料，缺乏相应的数字学习资源。

　　《西方文化教程》编写组在广泛调研的基础上，确定了 15 个有代表性的话题，旨在培养学生理解与分析各种文化现象的能力，提高他们的人文素养；教材兼具提高学生英语应用能力的目的，让学生在文化内容学习的同时掌握语言知识和语言技能，提高分析问题的能力、思辨能力和跨文化交际能力；纸质教材和数字资源相互补充，满足学生个性化学习需求，提高学生数字素养。

❖ 教材特色

1. 教材目标：文化知识传授与语言能力提高并重

　　目前许多西方文化类教材偏重于西方文化知识点的百科知识性介绍，练习设计比较单一，没有实现提高学生英语应用能力和跨文化交际能力的有机统一。教材是大学生学习英语的主要渠道之一，应兼顾知识传授和语言能力训练两大功能。只重视文化知识的传输而不重视英语语言能力的训练，只满足内容介绍而无语言技能的实践，学生则没有工具进行跨文化交际，英语学习也成了无本之木，无源之水。本教材练习设计分为两部分：一是知识类练习，有助于学生归纳总结所学相关文化的知识点；一是语言技能类练习，旨在提高学生的英语应用能力。

　　此外，教材充分考虑到了学生的应试压力（如大学英语四六级考试）和应用能力提高的双重需求，既设计了帮助学生提高快速阅读能力的信息匹配题，又设计了口语练习题和段落翻译题，旨在提高学生阅读能力的同时，提高其表达能力。教材还通过创造情景等，将学生所学的文化知识点内化，提高学生的跨文化交际能力。

2. 教材内容：选材新颖，语料真实

编写组在广泛调研的基础上精心挑选了 15 个话题，内容涵盖广泛而又喜闻乐见。选材大多来源于西方国家的主流报纸、杂志、网站或学术专著等，兼具时代性和实用性。编者根据中国大学生英语水平对相关语料进行适当改写，辅以图片，生动直观，充分调动学生学习的积极性，提高学习参与度。

3. 教材设计：线上线下相结合，资源丰富，可操作性强

教材配套丰富的线上学习资源，如视频、习题等，有效拓展知识的广度和深度，满足学生个性化学习需求。纸质教材和数字资源相互补充，教师可根据实际情况充分利用教材开展线上线下混合式教学，可操作性强。

❖ 教材框架

《西方文化教程》精心选择了神话、建筑、绘画、教育、文学、节日、礼仪、婚俗、时尚、美食、体育、歌剧、媒体、大选和英国脱欧等 15 个话题，既让学生了解西方文化的方方面面，又深度理解其文化渊源，提高学生的思辨能力和跨文化交际能力，树立文化自信。每个单元围绕一个话题设计了六个板块，具体如下：

Part I Goals: 列出本单元学习需要达到的目标。

Part II Warming-up: 该部分主要设计一些启发性的问题或小组活动，为单元的学习进行知识铺垫。

Part III Reading: 该部分精选风格不同的两篇文章，内容与单元主题相关。第一篇课文后面配有阅读理解、词汇语法、口语交际等相关练习；第二篇课文后面配有阅读理解题和翻译题。在教学中，教师可以灵活运用，课时充裕时可以在课堂精讲两篇，也可以根据教学实际选择其中一篇。

Part IV Exploring: 该部分基于前面阅读的内容设计场景，引导学生进行角色表演或开展其他口语活动，旨在将课文中所学的知识转化成能力，培养学生的跨文化能力。

Part V Mini-pedia: 该部分是与主题相关的小知识点补充。

Part VI Reflection: 该部分是学生自我学习效果的评价，旨在促使学生反思对本单元知识点的掌握程度，评价自己的学习效果，培养自主学习能力。

本教材所有编著人员都是大学英语一线教师，有丰富的教学经验。编写团队的具体分工如下：常娟负责第一单元和第六单元，王瑰负责第四单元，赵巧云负责第二单元和第七单元，陈虹波负责第三单元和第十二单元，周赟赟负责第五单元，陆小丽负责第八单元和第十五单元，曾靓婧负责第九单元，张淑芬负责第十单元和第十四单元，卢洁负责第十一单元和第十三单元。感谢王志茹教授、杨元刚教授、陶涛教授对本教材提出的宝贵意见和建议。

因编者水平有限，我们期待业内专家和广大师生的批评指正。

编者

2024 年 2 月于武汉

CONTENTS

UNIT 1
MYTHOLOGY

GOALS

1 To get some basic information about Greek mythology, such as the characters and the stories;

2 To become aware of the influence of Greek mythology;

3 To compare the stories of world creation in different cultures;

4 To acquire some words and expressions about Greek mythology.

Warming-up

Answer the following questions:

1. Do you know some Chinese myths and legends about the creation of the world and human beings? What are they?

2. According to Greek mythology, how was the world created?

3. Have you noticed the influence of Chinese legends and Greek mythology? Give some examples.

Reading

Passage One   Introduction to Mythology

❶ "Myth has two main functions," the poet and scholar Robert Graves wrote in 1955. "The first is to answer the sort of awkward questions that children ask, such as 'Who made the world? How will it end? Who was the first man? Where do souls go after death?'... The second function of myth is to justify an existing social system and account for traditional rites and customs." In ancient Greece, stories about gods and goddesses and heroes and monsters were an important part of everyday life. They explained everything from religious rituals to the weather, and they gave meaning to the world people saw around them.

Greek Mythology: Sources

❷ In Greek mythology, there is no single original text like the

Christian Bible or the Hindu Vedas that introduces all of the myths' characters and stories. Instead, the earliest Greek myths were part of an oral tradition that began in the Bronze Age, and their plots and themes unfolded gradually in the written literature of the **archaic** and classical periods. The poet Homer's 8th-century BC **epics** the *Iliad* and the *Odyssey*, for example, tell the story of the (mythical) Trojan War as a **divine** conflict as well as a human one. They do not, however, bother to introduce the gods and goddesses who are their main characters, since readers and listeners would already have been familiar with them.

archaic *adj.* 古代的；陈旧的

epic *n.* 史诗

divine *adj.* 神圣的；神的

❸　Around 700 BC, the poet Hesiod's *Theogony* offered the first written **cosmogony**, or origin story, of Greek mythology. The *Theogony* tells the story of the universe's journey from nothingness (Chaos, a **primeval void**) to being, and details an **elaborate** family tree of elements, gods and goddesses who evolved from Chaos and descended from Gaia (Earth), Uranus (Sky), Pontus (Sea) and Tartarus (the Underworld).

Theogony n.《神谱》

cosmogony *n.* 宇宙进化论；宇宙的起源

primeval *adj.* 原始的；初期的

void *n.* 空虚

elaborate *adj.* 详尽的；精心制作的

❹　Later Greek writers and artists used and elaborated upon these sources in their own work. For instance, mythological figures and events appear in the 5th-century plays of Aeschylus, Sophocles and Euripides and the **lyric** poems of Pindar. Writers such as the 2nd-century BC Greek **mythographer** Apollodorus of Athens and the 1st-century BC Roman historian Gaius Julius Hyginus **compiled** the ancient myths and legends for **contemporary** audiences.

lyric *adj.* 抒情的

mythographer *n.* 神话作者；神话讲述者

compile *v.* 编译；编制；编辑

contemporary *adj.* 同时代的；当代的

Greek Mythology: **The Olympians**

❺　At the center of Greek mythology is the **pantheon** of deities who were said to live on Mount Olympus, the highest mountain in Greece. From their **perch**, they ruled every aspect of human life. Olympian gods and goddesses looked like men and women (though they could change themselves into animals and other things) and were—as many myths **recounted**—vulnerable to human **foibles** and passions.

pantheon *n.* 万神殿

perch *n.* 高位；栖木

recount *v.* 叙述

foible *n.* 弱点；小缺点

❻ The twelve main Olympians are:

Zeus (Jupiter, in Roman mythology): the king of the gods of Mount Olympus (and father to many) and god of weather, law and fate

Hera (Juno): the queen of the gods of Mount Olympus and goddess of women and marriage

Aphrodite (Venus): goddess of beauty and love

Apollo (Apollo): god of **prophesy**, music and poetry, and knowledge

prophesy *n.* 预言

Ares (Mars): god of war

Artemis (Diana): goddess of hunting, animals and childbirth

Athena (Minerva): goddess of wisdom and warfare

Demeter (Ceres): goddess of agriculture and grain

Dionysos (Bacchus): god of wine, pleasure and **festivity**

festivity *n.* 欢庆；欢宴，庆典

Hephaestus (Vulcan): god of fire, metalworking and sculpture

Hermes (Mercury): god of travel, hospitality and trade and Zeus' personal messenger

Poseidon (Neptune): god of the sea

❼ Other gods and goddesses sometimes included in the **roster** of Olympians are:

roster *n.* 花名册

Hades (Pluto): god of the underworld

Hestia (Vesta): goddess of home and family

Eros (Cupid): god of sex and **minion** to Aphrodite

minion *n.* 宠儿；恋人

Greek Mythology: Heroes and Monsters

❽ Greek mythology does not just tell the stories of gods and goddesses, however. Human heroes—such as Heracles, the adventurer who performed 12 impossible labors for King Eurystheus (and was subsequently worshipped as a god for his accomplishment); Pandora, the first woman, whose curiosity brought evil to mankind; Pygmalion, the king who fell in love with an **ivory** statue; Arachne, the weaver who was turned into a spider for her arrogance; handsome Trojan prince Ganymede who became the **cupbearer** for the gods; Midas, the king with the golden touch; and Narcissus, the young man who fell in love with his own reflection—are just as significant. Monsters and "hybrids"

ivory *adj.* 乳白色的；象牙制的

cupbearer *n.* 上酒人，斟酒人

(human-animal forms) also feature **prominently** in the tales: the winged horse Pegasus, the horse-man Centaur, the lion-woman Sphinx and the bird-women Harpies, the one-eyed giant Cyclops, automatons (metal creatures given life by Hephaestus), manticores and unicorns, Gorgons, pygmies, Minotaurs, Satyrs and dragons of all sorts. Many of these creatures have become almost as well known as the gods, goddesses and heroes who share their stories.

prominently *adv.* 显著地

Greek Mythology: **Past and Present**

9 The characters, stories, themes and lessons of Greek mythology have shaped art and literature for thousands of years. They appear in Renaissance paintings such as Botticelli's *Birth of Venus* and Raphael's *Triumph of Gala-tea* and writings like Dante's *Inferno*; Romantic poetry and libretti; and scores of more recent novels, plays and films.

Inferno n. 《神曲》

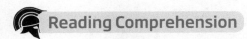

Reading Comprehension

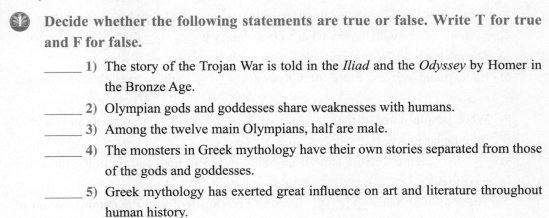

Decide whether the following statements are true or false. Write T for true and F for false.

_____ 1) The story of the Trojan War is told in the *Iliad* and the *Odyssey* by Homer in the Bronze Age.

_____ 2) Olympian gods and goddesses share weaknesses with humans.

_____ 3) Among the twelve main Olympians, half are male.

_____ 4) The monsters in Greek mythology have their own stories separated from those of the gods and goddesses.

_____ 5) Greek mythology has exerted great influence on art and literature throughout human history.

Answer the following questions with the information from the passage.

1) According to the passage, what are the two main functions of mythology?

2) What are the features of the earliest Greek myths?

3) Which work offered the first written introduction to a family tree for Greek mythology?

4) What do Olympian gods and goddesses look like?

5) According to the passage, besides gods and goddesses, who else is Greek mythology about?

Match the characters in Greek mythology with the correct information.

_____ 1) Aphrodite   A. fulfilled the 12 tasks for King Eurystheus.

_____ 2) Heracles   B. was crazy about his own image in the river.

_____ 3) Midas   C. was in charge of beauty and love.

_____ 4) Narcissus   D. was a horse with wings.

_____ 5) Pegasus   E. turned everything he touched into gold.

Language in Use

Fill in the blanks with the words from the word bank. Make changes when necessary.

myth	justify	namesake	elaboration	passion
divine	hospitality	contemporary	reflection	prominent

1) My next-door neighbour Sir Roger is very _____; he keeps his doors open.

2) Aristotle agrees with those who deny that slavery is _____ by war or conquest.

3) She made _____ preparations for the party, but no one showed up.

4) Educational systems more often than not _____ the essential nature of that society.

5) When people spoke of the _____, they were usually talking about an aspect of the mundane.

6) _____ achievements have been made in electronics and textiles processing industries.

7) There are too many _____, causing great difficulty to the administration of residential registration.

8) Another interesting group of names comes from _____.

9) China is a high-risk natural disaster country viewed historically and _____.

10) The city of Dallas was wild with excitement, and the fans were _____ and knowledgeable.

Translate the following paragraph into Chinese.

At the center of Greek mythology is the pantheon of deities who were said to live on Mount Olympus, the highest mountain in Greece. From their perch, they ruled every aspect of human life. Olympian gods and goddesses looked like men and women (though they could change themselves into animals and other things) and were—as many myths recounted—vulnerable to human foibles and passions.

 Oral Practice

 Read the passage again and summarize what you have learned about Greek mythology. You may use the following expressions.

Olympian gods and goddesses	source	epics	*Theogony*
heroes and monsters	literature	Renaissance	

Passage Two **The Creation**

❶ Perhaps the most confusing aspect of this myth is the **extensive** use of names that seem difficult to non-native Greek speakers to pronounce. This sometimes causes **frustration** and loss of track when trying to **establish** the continuing relationship between these characters in the birth of the world. So, please be patient and try to **associate** these names with the characters and events that took place.

extensive *adj.* 广泛的；大量的
frustration *n.* 挫折
establish *v.* 建立；创办

associate *v.* 联想；使联合

❷ It all started when Chaos, Gaea (Earth) and Eros started sleeping with each other, leading to the Gods. So, in Greek mythology, the creation of the world starts with the creation of the different classes of Gods. In this instance, the term "gods" refers to the characters that ruled the Earth (without necessarily possessing any divine **attributes**) until the "real" Gods, the Olympians, came.

attribute *n.* 属性；特质

So after this brief introduction, the next step is to examine the creation of the Gods (which really is the same thing, it's just that when you are interested in the creation of the world, you look at the very beginning of the creation of the Gods; while to examine the creation of the Gods, you have to look a little deeper).

❸ Hesiod's *Theogony* is one of the best introductions we have on the creation of the world. According to Hesiod, three major elements took part in the beginning of creation: Chaos, Gaea, and Eros. It is said that Chaos gave birth to Erebus and Night, while Uranus and Oceanus emerged from Gaea. Each child had a specific role, and Uranus' duty was to protect Gaea. Later, the two became a couple and were the first Gods to rule the world. They had twelve children known as the Titans, three known as the Cyclopes, and three Hecatoncheires, the hundred-handed Giants.

❹ The situation from here on, however, wasn't very peaceful. Uranus was a cruel father, afraid that he might be **overthrown** by his children; thus, he decided that his children belonged deep inside Gaea, hidden from himself and his kingdom. Gaea, **infuriated** with this arrangement, agreed at first, but later chose to help her children. She **devised** a plan to **rid** her children from their tyrant father and supplied her youngest child Cronus with a **sickle**. She then arranged a meeting for the two, in which Cronus cut off his father's **genitals**. The seed of Uranus which fell into the sea gave birth to Aphrodite, while his blood created the Fates, the Giants, and the Meliae nymphs.

overthrow *v.* 推翻；打倒

infuriate *v.* 激怒
devise *v.* 设计；想出
rid *v.* 使摆脱；使去掉
sickle *n.* 镰刀
genitals *n.* 生殖器

❺ Cronus **succeeded** his father in the throne and married his sister Rhea. He also freed his siblings and shared his kingdom with them. Oceanus was given the responsibility to rule over the sea and rivers, while Hyperion guided the Sun and the stars. When Cronus and Rhea started having their own children, Cronus was possessed by the very same fears that haunted his father.

succeed *v.* 继承；接替

❻ Cronus **eventually** decided that the best way to deal with this problem was to swallow all his children.

eventually *adv.* 最后，终于

❼   Of course, Rhea was very displeased and devised a plan to free her children. She managed to hide her youngest child, Zeus, from Cronus, by tricking him into swallowing a stone wrapped in infant clothes instead of the baby himself.

❽   The great Zeus was brought up by the Nymphs on Mount Dikti in the island of Crete. In order to cover the sound of his crying, the Kouretes danced and clashed their **shields**. As Zeus entered manhood, he gained the strength that few would dare dream of. He overthrew his father, and freed his siblings from his father's stomach, taking the throne and the rule of the universe.

shield *n.* 盾；防护物

Human Race

❾   According to the myths, the **immortal** Gods thought that it would be interesting to create beings similar to them, but mortal, in order to inhabit the earth. As soon as the mortals were created, Zeus, the leader of the Gods, ordered the two sons of the Titan Iapetus, Prometheus and Epimetheus, to give these beings various gifts in the hope that the mortals would evolve into interesting beings, able to amuse the Gods.

immortal *adj.* 不朽的；长生的

❿   So the two brothers started to divide the gifts among themselves in order to give them to the earth's inhabitants. Epimetheus gave the gift of beauty to some animals, **agility** on other animals, strength in others, and agility and speed to some. However, he left the human race defenseless, with no natural weapons in this new kingdom. Prometheus, who liked the human race, upon realizing what had happened, **promptly** distributed his own gifts to mankind. He stole reason from Athena, giving it to man. He then stole fire from the gates of Hephaestus, to keep human race warm. Prometheus then became the protector of the human race, and shared with it all the knowledge he had.

agility *n.* 敏捷，灵活；机敏

promptly *adv.* 迅速地，立即地；敏捷地

⓫   This new situation angered Zeus, for fire until now had been a gift only **reserved** for the Gods and he did not want the human race to **resemble** the Gods. Zeus' next step was to punish Prometheus. And a heavy punishment it was. Zeus chained Prometheus on a

reserve *v.* 储备；保留；预约
resemble *v.* 类似，像

peak in the Caucasus, which was believed to be at the end of the world. He had an eagle eat his liver every single day for thirty years. At the end of each day, Prometheus' liver would grow back again, so he would have to suffer all over again. After thirty years, Heracles **released** Prometheus from his nightmare.

release *v.* 释放；发射

Olympians

⑫　　The term Olympians refers to the twelve Gods of Mount Olympus, which is located in the northern central part of Greece. This mountain was believed to be **sacred** throughout ancient times and considered the highest point on earth. These Gods that ruled on Mount Olympus also ruled the lives of all mankind. Each and every single God (or Goddess) had their own character and **domain**. Gods in mythology were very human like. They had the strengths and weaknesses of mortals (as we know them today), truly made to represent each and every side of human nature. They also supported justice, as seen from their own point of view.

sacred *adj.* 神的；神圣的

domain *n.* 领域

⑬　　Gods even had children with mortals, which resulted in **demigods** like Heracles. The most amazing observation is how the **traits** of the Gods expressed human nature in its complete form. Strength, fear, unfaithfulness, love, admiration, beauty, hunting, farming, education; there was a God for every human activity and expression. These Gods weren't just ideal figures. They were beings with their own limitations. They expressed anger, jealousy and joy, just like humans. Each God ruled their own **realm**, apart from Zeus, who was **omnipotent** and ruled all.

demigod *n.* 半神半人
trait *n.* 特性，特点

realm *n.* 领域，范围；王国
omnipotent *adj.* 无所不能的，全能的

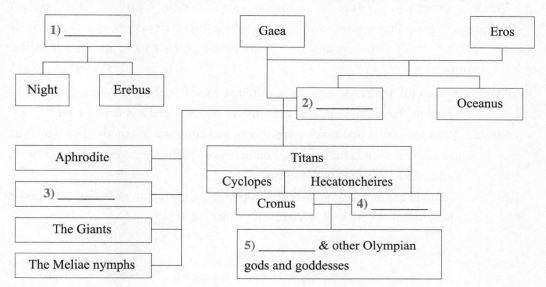

🎵 **Extended Activities**

🎵 **Complete the theogony based on the information from the passage.**

1) _____   Gaea   Eros

Night   Erebus   2) _____   Oceanus

Aphrodite   Titans

3) _____   Cyclopes   Hecatoncheires

The Giants   Cronus   4) _____

The Meliae nymphs   5) _____ & other Olympian gods and goddesses

🎵 **Answer the following questions based on the understanding of the passage.**

1) What is the relationship between Gaea and Uranus?

2) According to the passage, what were Hecatoncheires?

3) How was Cronus overthrown?

4) Why were humans created?

5) Who became the protector of human beings?

🎵 **Translate the following paragraphs into English.**

　　普罗米修斯是泰坦巨人之一。在宙斯与巨人的战争中，他站在新的奥林匹斯山神一边。他用黏土造出了第一个男人。雅典娜赋予了这个男人灵魂和神圣的生命。普罗米修斯还花费了很多时间和精力创造了火，并将之赠予人类。火使人成为万物之灵。

　　在这之后，举行了第一次神与人的联席会议。这个会议将决定烧烤过的动物的哪一部分该分给神，哪一部分该给人类。普罗米修斯切开一头牛，把它分成两部分：他把肉放在皮下，将骨头放在肥肉下。因为他知道自私的宙斯爱吃肥肉。宙斯看穿了他的把戏。普罗米修斯偏袒人类，这使宙斯感到不快。因此，他专横地把火从人类手中夺走。然而，普罗米修斯设法窃走了天火，偷偷地把它带给人类。

Exploring

Work in groups to prepare for a feature report for the Cultural Kaleidoscope column in the campus newspaper to introduce the differences and similarities between myths of different cultures. Your group work can be divided into the following steps.

Step 1 Search for myths and legends in different countries about the stories like world creation, the origin of human beings, love between god and humans, etc.

Step 2 Read the stories and make comparisons and contrasts in groups, then work out the similarities and differences. You may even go further to explore the cultural differences embodied in the stories.

Step 3 Compile and improve your feature report. Don't forget to add some pictures to illustrate what you want to share with your readers.

Mini-pedia

Do You Know?

Many consumer products get their names from Greek mythology. Nike sneakers are the namesake of the goddess of victory, for example, and the website Amazon.com is named after the race of mythical female warriors. Many high school, college and professional sports teams (Titans, Spartans and Trojans, for instance) also get their names from mythological sources.

 **Reflection**

Achievements	Yes	No
I am familiar with some Greek myths and the characters.		
I am aware of the influences of Greek mythology in the human history.		
I have understood that there are both similarities and differences between myths and legends of different cultures.		
I have acquired some useful words and expressions related to Greek mythology.		

UNIT 2
ARCHITECTURE

GOALS

1. To know the main styles of western architecture;
2. To know the different features of the main western architectural styles;
3. To know some famous architects;
4. To acquire some words and expressions about western architecture.

Warming-up

Answer the following questions:

1. What do you know about the American architect Jeanne Gang?

2. How much do you know about Aqua?

3. What architectural styles do you know? What are their features?

Reading

Passage One Wave Effect

By Paul Goldberger

❶ Aqua—a new, eighty-two-story apartment tower in the center of Chicago—is made of the same tough, brawny materials as most skyscrapers: metal, concrete, and lots of glass. But the architect, Jeanne Gang, a forty-five-year-old Chicagoan, has figured out a way to give it soft, silky lines, like **draped** fabric. She started with a fairly conventional rectangular glass slab, then transformed it by wrapping it on all four sides with wafer-thin, curving concrete balconies, describing a different shape on each floor. Gang turned the **façade** into an **undulating** landscape of bending, flowing concrete, as if the wind were blowing **ripples** across the surface of the building. You know this tower is huge and solid, but it feels malleable, its exterior pulsing with a gentle rhythm.

❷ The building would be an achievement for any architect, but Gang, who has run her own firm since 1997, had never designed a skyscraper before and happened into this one almost by accident.

drape v. (随便地) 披上，披盖；悬挂

façade n. 建筑物正面
undulating adj. 波动的
ripple n. 涟漪，细浪

A couple of years ago, she was seated at a dinner next to Jim Lowenberg, a developer who had built a number of **mediocre** condominium towers in a huge development over the old Illinois Central rail yards, known as Lakeshore East. A prime site in the project remained, Lowenberg told her, and he envisioned doing something more ambitious there. He liked Gang and offered her a shot.

mediocre *adj.* 平庸的；平凡的

❸ A lot of attention—in Chicago, at least—has been given to the fact that Aqua is the tallest building in the world designed by a woman. That's nice for Gang, but beside the point, and dwelling on it leads too easily to predictable interpretations of skyscrapers as symbols of male identity. Gang's achievement has more to do with freeing us from such silliness. Her building is most **compelling** as an example of architecture that is practical and affordable enough to please real-estate developers and stirring enough to please critics. Not many buildings like that get made at any height, or by architects of either gender.

compelling *adj.* 引人注目的；令人赞赏的

❹ Furthermore, the success of Aqua isn't just that Gang figured out a smart, low-budget way of turning an ordinary glass condo tower into something that looks exciting. The design is anchored in common sense in two ways that aren't immediately apparent, making the building, from a technical point of view, even more remarkable than it looks. The balcony overhangs of the façade serve an environmental purpose, shading apartments from the hot summer sun. More **ingenious** still, they protect the building from the force of wind, one of the most difficult challenges in skyscraper engineering. The landscape of rolling hills and valleys created by the balconies effectively confuses the heavy Chicago winds, giving them no clear path. The wind is broken up so much that the building didn't require a device known as a "tuned mass **damper**"—a mass weighing hundreds of tons that engineers place at the top of tall buildings to stabilize them against the vibrations and sway caused by the force of wind. And using the curves to **dissipate** the wind gave Gang a bonus: she was able to put balconies on every floor, all the way up. Usually, condominiums sixty or seventy floors above the street don't have balconies, because it's just too windy up there to go outside.

ingenious *adj.* 独具创造力的；巧妙的

damper *n.* 减音器；减震器

dissipate *v.* 驱散

⑤ Female architects share a high interest in modern design combined with a low interest in ideology. They approach design less as an opportunity to demonstrate a set of ideas than as a way of answering a series of questions about the nature of a place, a client, or a function. "I like to do research about a place, about materials, and about a program," Gang told me. "The longer I can delay coming up with a form, the better. Developers don't always like that, but it's the part I like the most." In the case of Aqua, she experimented with several ideas before she settled on making a façade out of what she calls the "built **contours**" of undulating concrete balconies. Gang worked for Rem Koolhaas in Rotterdam for two years after she got her architecture degree, at Harvard, but she considered becoming an engineer before she decided to be an architect, and she thinks primarily in terms of what is buildable. Still, she is passionate about what her buildings look like—"I have a preference for light structure, for things that look light, almost fragile," she told me—and as capable of **obsessing** over a single detail as Norman Foster. But she seems determined to approach her projects without preconceived notions of what they should look like. "I don't think I could have sketched Aqua on Day One," she said.

contour *n.* 外形，轮廓

obsess *v.* 迷住；使着迷

⑥ When I went to Chicago to see Aqua, Gang took me through the building, but she seemed more interested in making sure I got to see two new projects that were barely larger than the biggest Aqua apartments: a community center and a video-and-film production center for Columbia College, both on the South Side. The community center has a façade made up of several layers of different types of concrete, added unevenly one atop the other, so that the exterior looks like a **gargantuan** sand painting, an abstract composition in gray and beige—another instance of a powerful aesthetic statement achieved with conventional materials used in an unconventional way. At Columbia, an arts college housed in a series of old buildings, Gang's center, the first entirely new structure that the college has built, is an **exuberant** building of concrete and glass whose interior is laid out so as to emphasize framed views from one area to another: Gang approached the project thinking in terms of how a director might frame shots through a camera. She also tinted some of the glass in the façade to resemble the blocks of color in a television test pattern.

gargantuan *adj.* 巨大的，庞大的

exuberant *adj.* 华丽的；丰盛的

7   That's the sort of idea that could be a **gimmick**, but Gang is good enough to pull it off. She designs by trying to identify with the client, and coming up with something that she wouldn't do for anyone else. For an environmental center, also on the South Side, she decided to construct most of the building out of recycled material, and ended up using not only recycled steel for the exterior cladding but recycled blue jeans as an **insulating** material. For a housing complex in Hyderabad, she is trying to find a way to reinterpret the traditional Indian courtyard house in high-rise form.

gimmick *n.* 花招；噱头

insulating *adj.* 绝缘的

8   Gang has no interest in establishing a look that marks her buildings as hers. Her instincts are modern, but style alone doesn't shape her work; materials, technology, and an ongoing attempt to see from the perspective of the people who will use the buildings mean much more to her. "You know, a lot of architects get into **fetishized** objects," she said to me. "But when you can design anything you want without actually having to make it, you do wild things that can't work. And that's not what I want to do."

fetishize *v.* 迷恋，痴迷

Reading Comprehension

Decide whether the following statements are true or false. Write T for true and F for false.

    _____ 1) Gang decided to be an architect soon after she got her architecture degree at Harvard.

    _____ 2) The overhanging balconies of the façade can protect the building from the force of the wind in addition to shading the apartment from the hot summer sun.

    _____ 3) The eighty-two-story apartment tower, Aqua, has no distinctive differences from most skyscrapers.

    _____ 4) Gang was determined to use recycled material in the construction of most of her buildings.

    _____ 5) The architect, Jeanne Gang, had successfully designed many skyscrapers before she set about designing Aqua.

    _____ 6) Using curves to disperse the wind enabled Gang to put balconies on every floor, which was usually impossible for buildings sixty or seventy floors at that time.

Complete the sentences with the information from the passage.

1) The architect Jeanne Gang turned the façade of Aqua into a wavy landscape of bending, flowing concrete, as if the wind were blowing _____ across the surface of the building.

2) Gang's achievement has freed people from the silly interpretation that skyscrapers are the symbols of _____.

3) The overhanging balconies of the façade break up the heavy Chicago winds so that the building doesn't need a device called a "tuned mass damper" to stabilize it against the _____ caused by the force of wind.

4) The community center, another new project by Gang, has a façade composed of several layers of different types of concrete and its _____ looks like a huge sand painting, which makes it another example of powerful _____ statement achieved with conventional materials in unconventional ways.

5) Gang decided to construct most of the building out of recycled material; for example, she used recycled steel for the exterior _____ and recycled blue jeans as a(n) _____ material.

Each of the following statements contains information given in one of the paragraphs in the passage. Identify the paragraph from which the information is derived and put the corresponding number in the space provided.

_____ 1) Gang likes to do research about a place, about materials and programs while developers often don't like to.

_____ 2) Gang's instincts are modern; however, her style alone doesn't mark her work, for materials, technology, etc. mean much more to her.

_____ 3) Gang had never designed a skyscraper before and she got the opportunity to build Aqua tower almost by chance.

_____ 4) Although Aqua was built by using the same materials as most skyscrapers, Gang worked out a way to make it look like draped fabric with soft, silky lines.

_____ 5) Gang made sure the author went to see two new projects, which were larger than the biggest Aqua apartments when the author went to visit Aqua in Chicago.

_____ 6) The overhanging balconies of the façade protect the building from the force of the wind, which is one of the most difficult challenges in skyscraper engineering.

_____ 7) Gang was determined to use recycled material to construct most of the building for an environment center on the South Side.

_____ 8) Aqua is the tallest building in the world designed by a female architect.

 **Language in Use**

4 **Fill in the blanks with the words from the word bank. Make changes when necessary.**

fetishize	drape	undulate	compelling	ingenious
dissipate	preconceive	gargantuan	exuberant	insulating

1) Tourists forget their _____ ideas as soon as they visit our country.
2) The director used _____ devices to keep the audience in suspense.
3) When you feel tension building, find something fun to do. You'll find that the stress you feel will _____ and your thoughts will become clearer.
4) I'll _____ this coat around your shoulders to keep you warm.
5) A _____ pair of towers dominate the skyline of Malaysia's capital Kuala Lumpur. The mighty Petronas Towers scale 88 floors to a breath-taking 1,476 feet, nearly a third of a mile high.
6) They would have been more of an economic powerhouse if they didn't _____ authoritarian governance, but I would be less afraid of them if they did open up.
7) The Boao Plaza, the main conference venue, is a structure that is open on all sides with the _____ roof resembling a seagull ready to take wing.
8) A state could not contravene the freedom of contract unless there were obvious and _____ reasons for exercising the police power.
9) A rigid, clear thermoplastic polymer that can be molded into objects or made into a foam that is used to _____ refrigerators.
10) Mark Twain's sense of humor, like Dickens', is based on an _____ appreciation of language.

5 **Translate the following paragraph into Chinese.**

Gang has no interest in establishing a look that marks her buildings as hers. Her instincts are modern, but style alone doesn't shape her work; materials, technology, and an ongoing attempt to see from the perspective of the people who will use the buildings mean much more to her. "You know, a lot of architects get into fetishized objects," she said to me. "But when you can design anything you want without actually having to make it, you do wild things that can't work. And that's not what I want to do."

Oral Practice

Work in groups and discuss how to strike a balance between achieving practical purposes and aesthetic representations in the construction of a building.

Passage Two The History of Western Architecture

By Jackie Craven

Monoliths, Mounds, and Prehistoric Structures

① Prehistoric builders moved earth and stone into **geometric** forms, creating our earliest human-made structures. We don't know why primitive people began building geometric structures. Archaeologists can only guess that prehistoric people looked to the heavens to imitate the circular forms of the sun and the moon, using that natural shape in their creations of earth mounds and **monolithic** henges.

geometric *adj.* 几何图形的

monolithic *adj.* 独块巨石的; 庞大的

② Many fine examples of well-preserved prehistoric architecture are found in southern England. Stonehenge in Amesbury, United Kingdom is a well-known example of the prehistoric stone circle. Nearby Silbury Hill, also in Wiltshire, is the largest man-made, prehistoric earthen mound in Europe. At 30 meters high and 160 meters wide, the gravel mound is layers of soil, mud, and grass, with dug pits and tunnels of chalk and clay. Completed in the late Neolithic period, approximately 2400 BC, its architects were a Neolithic civilization in Britain.

3050 BC–900 BC: Ancient Egypt

③ The pyramid form was a marvel of engineering that allowed ancient Egyptians to build enormous structures.

④   Wood was not widely available in the **arid** Egyptian landscape. Houses in ancient Egypt were made with blocks of sun-baked mud. Flooding of the Nile River and the ravages of time destroyed most of these ancient homes.

arid *adj.* 干燥的

⑤   Much of what we know about ancient Egypt is based on great temples and tombs, which were made with granite and limestone and decorated with **hieroglyphics**, carvings, and brightly colored frescoes. The ancient Egyptians didn't use **mortar**, so the stones were carefully cut to fit together.

hieroglyphics *n.* 象形文字
mortar *n.* 砂浆

⑥   The development of the pyramid form allowed Egyptians to build enormous tombs for their kings. The sloping walls could reach great heights because their weight was supported by the wide pyramid base. An innovative Egyptian named Imhotep is said to have designed one of the earliest of the massive stone monuments, the Step Pyramid of Djoser (2667 BC–2648 BC).

⑦   Builders in ancient Egypt didn't use load-bearing arches. Instead, columns were placed close together to support the heavy stone **entablature** above. Brightly painted and elaborately carved, the columns often mimicked palms, papyrus plants, and other plant forms.

entablature *n.* (古典建筑的)
柱上楣构，檐部

850 BC–476 AD: Classical

⑧   The classical architecture of ancient Greece and Rome has shaped the way we build today. From the rise of ancient Greece until the fall of the Roman Empire, great buildings were constructed according to precise rules. The Roman architect Marcus Vitruvius, who lived during the first century BC, believed that builders should use mathematical principles when constructing temples. "For without symmetry and proportion no temple can have a regular plan", Vitruvius wrote in his famous **treatise** *De Architectura*, or *Ten Books on Architecture*.

treatise *n.* 专著

⑨   In his writings, Marcus Vitruvius introduced the classical orders, which defined column styles and entablature designs used in classical architecture. The earliest classical orders were Doric, Ionic, and Corinthian.

⑩   More than 1,500 years after the Roman architect Vitruvius wrote his important book, the Renaissance architect Giacomo da Vignola outlined Vitruvius' ideas in a treatise titled *The Five Orders of Architecture*. Published in 1563, this book became a guide for builders throughout western Europe.

⑪   In 1570, another Renaissance architect, Andrea Palladio, used the new technology of movable type to publish *I Quattro Libri dell' Architettura*, or *The Four Books of Architecture*. In this book, Palladio showed how classical rules could be used not just for grand temples but also for private villas. Palladio's ideas spread across Europe and into the New World, giving rise to a variety of **neoclassical** styles.

neoclassical *adj.* 新古典主义的

527 AD–565 AD: Byzantine

⑫   Eastern and Western traditions combined in the sacred buildings of the Byzantine period. Buildings were designed with a central dome that eventually rose to new heights by using engineering practices refined in the Middle East. This era of architectural history was transitional and transformational. What is Byzantine architecture? Take a look at early Christian churches to find out what makes it so important.

800 AD–1200 AD: Romanesque

⑬   Even as the Roman Empire faded, Roman ideas reached far across Europe. Built between 1070 and 1120 AD, the **Basilica** of St. Sernin is a good example of this transitional architecture, with a Byzantine-domed apse and an added Gothic-like **steeple**. The floor plan is that of the Latin cross, Gothic-like again, with a high altar and tower at the cross intersection. Constructed of stone and brick, St. Sernin in Toulouse, France, is on the pilgrimage route to Santiago de Compostela.

basilica *n.* 长方形教堂

steeple *n.* 尖塔；尖顶

⑭   Romanesque buildings have regional variations, but share many common features, most notably the prominent rounded arch.

1100–1450: Gothic

⑮   Early in the 12th century, new ways of building meant that cathedrals and other large buildings could soar. Gothic architecture became characterized by the architectural elements that allowed these great heights—pointed arches, ribbed vaulting, and flying **buttresses**. In addition, elaborate stained glass took the place of walls that no longer were used to support high ceilings. **Gargoyles** and other sculptures also enabled practical and decorative functions.

buttress *n.* 扶壁
gargoyle *n.*（哥特式建筑上）承溜口，怪兽状滴水嘴

⑯   Gothic architecture began mainly in France where builders began to adapt the earlier Romanesque style. Builders were also influenced by the pointed arches and elaborate stonework of **Moorish** architecture in Spain. One of the earliest Gothic buildings was the **ambulatory** of the abbey of St. Denis in France, built between 1140 and 1144. Many of the world's most well-known sacred places are from this period in architectural history, including Chartres Cathedral and Paris' Notre Dame Cathedral in France and Dublin's St. Patrick's Cathedral and Adare Friary in Ireland.

Moorish *adj.* 摩尔人风格的
ambulatory *n.*（尤指教堂、寺院）回廊，走道

⑰   Originally, Gothic architecture was known as the French style. During the Renaissance, after the French style had fallen out of fashion, artisans mocked it. They coined the word Gothic to suggest that French style buildings were the **crude** work of German (Goth) barbarians. Although the label wasn't accurate, the name Gothic remained.

crude *adj.* 粗制的

1400–1600: Renaissance

⑱   During the Renaissance, architects were inspired by the carefully proportioned buildings of classical Greece and Rome. Italian Renaissance master Andrea Palladio helped awaken a passion for classical architecture when he designed beautiful, highly symmetrical villas such as La Rotonda.

1600–1830: Baroque

⑲ Early in the 1600s, an elaborate new architectural style **lavished** buildings. What became known as Baroque was characterized by complex shapes, extravagant ornaments, opulent paintings, and bold contrasts.

lavish v. 滥施；慷慨给予

⑳ Architecture was only one expression of the Baroque style. In music, famous names included Bach, Handel, and Vivaldi. In the art world, Caravaggio, Bernini, Rubens, Rembrandt, Vermeer, and Velázquez are remembered. Famous inventors and scientists of the day include Blaise Pascal and Isaac Newton.

1730–1925: Neoclassicism

㉑ In 1563, Renaissance architect Giacomo da Vignola outlined the principles of classical architecture in a treatise titled *The Five Orders of Architecture*. A few years later, another Renaissance architect, Andrea Palladio, described his own approach to classical architecture in *The Four Books of Architecture*.

㉒ These books were widely translated and inspired builders throughout western Europe. By the 1700s, European architects were turning away from elaborate Baroque and Rococo styles and in favor of restrained neoclassical approaches. Orderly, symmetrical neoclassical architecture reflected the intellectual awakening among the middle and upper classes in Europe during the period historians often call the Enlightenment. In the late 1700s and early 1800s, the newly-formed United States also drew upon classical ideals to construct grand government buildings and smaller private homes.

1905–1930: Neo-Gothic

㉓ In the early 20th century, skyscrapers borrowed details from medieval Gothic architecture. The Tribune Tower in Chicago which was built in 1924 is an example of Neo-Gothic design. Raymond Hood and John Howells were selected over many other architects to design the building. Their Neo-Gothic design may have appealed to the judges because it reflected a conservative (some critics said "regressive") approach. The façade of the Tribune Tower is studded with rocks collected from great buildings around the world.

24 Gothic Revival was a Victorian style inspired by Gothic cathedrals and other medieval architecture. In the early 20th century, Gothic Revival ideas were applied to modern skyscrapers. Twentieth Century Gothic Revival buildings are often called Neo-Gothic.

25 Neo-Gothic buildings have many of these features: strong vertical lines and a sense of great height; pointed windows with decorative **tracery**; gargoyles and other carvings; **pinnacles**.

tracery *n.* 窗花格

pinnacle *n.* 尖塔

1900–Present: Modernist Styles

26 Modernism was not just another style—it presented a new way of thinking. Modernist architecture emphasizes function. It attempts to provide for specific needs rather than imitate nature. The roots of Modernism may be found in the work of Berthold Lubetkin (1901–1990), a Russian architect who settled in London and founded a group called "Tecton". The Tecton architects believed in applying scientific and analytical methods to design. Their stark buildings ran counter to expectations and often seemed to defy gravity.

27 Modernist architecture has these features: little or no ornamentation; factory-made parts; man-made materials such as metal and concrete; emphasis on function; rebellion against traditional styles.

1972–Present: Postmodernism

28 Postmodern architecture evolved from the modernist movement yet contradicts many of the modernist ideas. Combining new ideas with traditional forms, postmodernist buildings may startle, surprise, and even amuse. Familiar shapes and details are used in unexpected ways. Buildings may **incorporate** symbols

incorporate *v.* 使并入

to make a statement or simply to delight the viewer. Philip Johnson's AT&T Headquarters is often cited as an example of Postmodernism.

 Extended Activities

Each of the following statements contains information given in one of the paragraphs in the passage. Identify the paragraph from which the information is derived and put the corresponding number in the space provided.

_____ 1) The Roman architect Marcus Vitruvius believed that there couldn't be a regular plan for temples without symmetry and proportion.

_____ 2) Gothic Revival ideas were applied to modern skyscrapers in the early 20th century.

_____ 3) After the French style was out of fashion, artisans mocked it by coining the word Gothic to suggest that French style buildings were the crude work of German (Goth) barbarians.

_____ 4) The wide pyramid base could support the high sloping walls which allowed Egyptians to build enormous tombs for their kings.

_____ 5) Modernist architecture gives emphasis on function and tries to provide specific needs instead of imitating nature.

_____ 6) Constructed of stone and brick, the Basilica of St. Sernin has a Byzantine-domed apse and an added Gothic-like steeple.

_____ 7) Archaeologists guess that prehistoric builders imitated the circular forms of the sun and the moon in their creation of geometric structures.

_____ 8) There are also expressions of the Baroque style in music and art.

_____ 9) By the 1700s, European architects were tired of elaborate Baroque and Rococo styles and in favor of restrained neoclassical approaches.

_____ 10) The Renaissance architect Palladio indicated in his book that classical rules could also be used for the construction of private villas besides grand temples.

Answer the following questions based on the understanding of the passage.

1) What made it possible for ancient Egyptians to build enormous tombs for their kings?

2) What are the architectural features of Gothic style?

3) What are the features of Neo-Gothic buildings?

4) What is Baroque style characterized by?

5) What are the three earliest classical orders and who put forward the five orders of architecture?

 Translate the following paragraph into English.

建筑是一门出于实用和象征的双重目的，通过组织和利用空间来实现设计结构的艺术和科学。因为建筑源于人类的需求和愿望，所以它可以清楚地传达文化价值。在所有的视觉艺术中，建筑最直接地影响了我们的生活，因为它在很多方面决定了我们生存的环境特征。一幢建筑物必须实现空间、质量、纹理、线条、光线、颜色等要素的和谐搭配。建筑师们创造出来的不单纯是建筑物，还为人们带来了灵感和喜悦。由于建筑能为人类提供栖身之处，丰富人们的生存空间，改善人们的居所环境，适应不同气候的变化，而且经济上具有可行性，所以它们有助于提高人类的生活质量。

 # Exploring

Work in groups and answer the following questions.

1) What are the major features of modern and postmodern architectures?
2) What are the typical structures of modern and postmodern architectures respectively?
3) Make a comparison between modern and postmodern architectures and tell the differences between them.

 # Mini-pedia

Greek Architectural Orders

An architectural order describes a style of building. In classical architecture, each order is readily identifiable by means of its proportions and profiles as well as by various aesthetic details. The classical orders—described by the labels Doric, Ionic, and Corinthian—do not merely serve as descriptors for the remains of ancient buildings but as an index to the architectural and aesthetic development of Greek architecture itself.

The Doric Order

The Doric order is the earliest of the three Classical orders of architecture and represents an important moment in Mediterranean architecture when monumental construction made the transition from impermanent materials—like wood—to permanent materials, namely stone. The Doric order is characterized by a plain, unadorned column capital and a column that rests directly on the stylobate of the temple without a base. The Doric entablature includes a frieze composed of triglyphs—vertical plaques with three divisions—and metopes—square spaces for either painted or sculpted decoration. The columns are fluted and are of sturdy, if not stocky, proportions.

The Ionic Order

As its name suggests, the Ionic order originated in Ionia, a coastal region of central Anatolia—today Turkey—where a number of ancient Greek settlements were located. Volutes, scroll-like ornaments, characterize the Ionic capital, and a base supports the column, unlike the Doric order. The monumental temple dedicated to Hera on the island of Samos, built by the architect Rhoecus, was the first of the great Ionic buildings, although it was destroyed by fire in short order.

The Ionic order is notable for its graceful proportions, which produce a more slender and elegant profile than the Doric order. The ancient Roman architect Vitruvius compared the Doric module to a sturdy, male body, while the Ionic was possessed of more graceful, feminine proportions.

The Corinthian Order

The Corinthian order is both the latest and the most elaborate of the classical orders of architecture. This order was employed in both Greek and Roman architecture with minor variations and gave rise, in turn, to the Composite order. As the name suggests, the origins of the order were connected in antiquity with the Greek city-state of Corinth,

where, according to the architectural writer Vitruvius, the sculptor Callimachus drew a set of acanthus leaves surrounding a votive basket. In archaeological terms, the earliest known Corinthian capital comes from the Temple of Apollo Epicurius at Bassae and dates to c. 427 BCE.

The defining element of the Corinthian order is its elaborate, carved capital, which incorporates even more vegetal elements than the Ionic order does. The Romans favored the Corinthian order, perhaps due to its slender properties. The order is employed in numerous notable Roman architectural monuments, including the Temple of Mars Ultor, the Pantheon in Rome, and the Maison Carrée in Nîmes.

 **Reflection**

Achievements	Yes	No
I have got to know the main styles of western architecture.		
I have got to know the different features of the main western architectural styles.		
I have gained some knowledge about some famous architects.		
I have acquired some useful words and expressions related to architecture.		

UNIT 3
WESTERN PAINTING

◇

GOALS

1 To know some basic facts and values of western paintings;

2 To understand general schools and traditions in western painting history;

3 To become aware of the differences between traditional Chinese paintings and western paintings;

4 To acquire some words and expressions about western paintings.

Warming-up

Answer the following questions:

1. How much do you know about the painter Paul Cézanne?

2. How much do you know about the terms "Impressionism", "Cubism" and "Expressionism"?

3. Who are the representatives of the school of Impressionism?

Reading

Passage One   Paul Cézanne

① Cézanne was born in Aix-en-Provence on January 19, 1839, the son of a wealthy banker whose allowance enabled Cézanne to continue producing works that brought in no money or critical approval. In truth, the young man had no obvious gift for painting but was **grudgingly** sent to study art in Paris. Zola was a boyhood friend, and in Paris Cézanne mixed with the more progressive element, including the Impressionists, though painting himself in a romantic, florid and heavy manner. From 1872, however, under Pissarro's **tutelage**, Cézanne began to paint out of doors, and exhibited with the Impressionists in 1874 and 1877. When his work attracted the harshest criticism, Cézanne drifted away from the group and spent more of his time in Aix-en-Provence. He quarreled bitterly with Zola in 1886 over the novelist's portrayal of a failed painter, becoming more socially isolated than ever. In his forties, Cézanne married Marie-Hortense Fiquet, his long-

grudgingly *adv.* 勉强地

tutelage *n.* 监护；指导

suffering model/mistress, and achieved financial independence when his father died a year later. Marie-Hortense left him shortly afterwards, however, and Cézanne moved in with his sister and mother.

② So continued Cézanne's quiet existence, **monastically** devoted to paintings that continually disappointed him and which he often destroyed. His contacts with the earlier Impressionists were **tenuous**, but Cézanne's commitment to his art became legendary, attracting the interest of van Gogh and Gauguin. Following an exhibition arranged for him by the Parisian art dealer Ambroise Vollard in 1895, Cézanne became better known, and in 1904 his work featured in a major official exhibition. Young artists traveled down to see him, and the last years to his death in Aix on October 22, 1906 were comparatively happy. Marie-Hortense died in 1922. She was disinherited by Cézanne, but received a settlement from their son, which was gambled away. The son inherited the entire estate and died in 1947.

③ Cézanne was a slow worker, putting a great deal of thought into each **stroke** of the brush—as most painters do, but by him taken to heroic lengths. Composition, color balance and a host of other matters that the Academy had taught painters to work out before putting brush to canvas was abandoned in favor of a direct method that would nonetheless (if only occasionally) produce a successful painting. Each brush stroke not only represented "something" of what he saw, but also took account of all previous brushstrokes in aiming for two things: a sense of the third dimension that did not involve perspective, and an integration of elements into the plane of the canvas. Both are difficult objectives, and Cézanne's work often shows **provisional**, repeated attempts to get things right—in this "bungling" (as Sickert called it) quite different from artists who copied him (e.g. Roger Fry) or the Cubists (e.g. Braque and Gris) who just took the simplifications and made bold designs with them.

monastically *adv.* 僧院地

tenuous *adj.* 稀薄的；贫乏的

stroke *n.* 笔画

provisional *adj.* 即兴的

④ *Madame Cézanne* is an unusually pleasing work of Cézanne's early maturity. The color scheme is **triadic**—secondary triadic, as the colors are not primary but in fact quite **muddy**. The third dimension is given by overlap (the sitter partly obscures the chair and wall behind) and by tone. The dress billows out towards us, but is rendered ambiguous in depth by dabs of light gray to the extreme left and right of its fabric, bringing areas of shadow **arbitrarily** towards the light. The curve of the bust, and the shadow it casts give the sitter's **torso** some modeling, but again it's not consistent: the (sitter's) left breast is up and the right is down. As expected, the sitter's hands are further back than the front of the dress, and closer to us than the head, but we find on looking closer at the head, that it perversely seems in some way closer to us than the dress, probably because it's lighter and pinker (color perspective) than those olive-gray bands. In short, the rendering of the third dimension is only local, and this wavering effect creates an undulating surface not far detached from the canvas plane.

triadic *adj.* 三合一的

muddy *adj.* 模糊的

arbitrarily *adv.* 任意地

torso *n.* 躯干

⑤ The sitter's head is left as an assembly of **curved** planes, which looks incompletely finished or "knobby" by the earlier expectations of art, but is here part of Cézanne's purpose, which is to replace traditional impressions of depth by an **interlocking** complex of tiny planes. For a similar purpose, parts of the wall behind and the sofa are given patches of lighter tone, though the sofa on the viewer's left practically merges with the **tiling**: there is no sense of depth here. The sofa is given a dark outline on the right, however, and its shape is distorted, appearing as a separate curve on the other side of the head. The arms make a cross with the ends of the jacket (and distorted, the left forearm is longer than the right), and that cross is echoed in the wall tiles. Part of that cross also forms part of the compositional device of curves—a very flat curve in the hoop of the dress and less so in the top of the sofa. **Distortions** are being made for decorative effects.

curved *adj.* 弯曲的

interlocking *adj.* 连锁的

tiling *n.* 瓷砖；盖瓦

distortion *n.* 变形，扭曲

⑥ Cézanne rarely painted flowers as they were apt to wilt before his deliberations were complete, but he did depict apples **aplenty**, here convincingly modeled in the third dimension but

aplenty *adv.* 丰富地

enclosed in **taut** circular outlines. The flowers of the Chinese **primrose** are also circular, as is the right (to us) side of their enclosing pot—a distortion from the ellipse we would expect. The whole plant in fact looks flat and anything but **succulent**, yet seems to lean out towards us. The cloth and apples are ambiguous in the third dimension: receding comfortably into the distance in the left corner of the table, but being spilled **vertiginously** along the table edge near us. The painting is becoming angular, even formulaic, but is preserved from the abstract by the colors of the apples and their modeling.

taut *adj.* 拉紧的

primrose *n.* 报春花

succulent *adj.* 多汁的，多水分的

vertiginously *adv.* 旋转地

7 In this late work Cézanne has moved further to abstraction: simplified shapes, an only-hinted-at solidity, a thrusting energy to the rock forms, and the almost complete loss of the third dimension: the overhanging trees on the right seem as clouds, distant as Mont Sainte-Victoire itself. The brush strokes are now laid like overlapping tiles, but the composition is conventional: three planes (trees, quarry wall and mountain), a **rectilinear** grid and a gentle swirling motion brought out by the rounded rock forms, the trees to the right and the shape of Mont Sainte-Victoire.

rectilinear *adj.* 形成直线的

8 Cézanne's art is an inspiration and a warning. **Dogged** persistence paid off, though never before had anyone so **devoid** of commanding flair and skill become a painter of the first rank. A warning because Cézanne is prized for what he led to—short-lived movements, promotion by critics, galleries and dealers, and investment opportunities for the wealthy as the traditional old masters were increasingly removed to public collections. It's Cézanne's intense devotion to his craft that distinguishes his work from those of followers, but—as with Monet—the paintings are far less novel than art critics sometimes assert. Nonetheless, the very action of painting, the thought that goes into each and every brushstroke, became important for one line of development, that of abstract painting. And, once severed from the need to create a photographic likeness, the canvas could serve as the battle ground for novel ideas as to what painting could and should be: **Cubism** and Expressionism.

dogged *adj.* 顽固的

devoid *adj.* 缺乏的

Cubism *n.* 立体主义

Reading Comprehension

1. Decide whether the following statements are true or false. Write T for true and F for false.

_____ 1) In truth, the young man didn't have much of a gift for painting but was grudgingly sent to study art in Paris.

_____ 2) His contacts with the earlier Impressionists were frequent.

_____ 3) *Madame Cézanne* is an unusually pleasing work of Cézanne's early maturity.

_____ 4) In this late work Cézanne has moved further to abstraction: simplified shapes, an only-hinted-at solidity, a thrusting energy to the rock forms, and the almost complete loss of the third dimension: the overhanging trees on the right seem as clouds, distant as Mont Sainte-Victoire itself.

_____ 5) It's Cézanne's intense devotion to his craft that distinguishes his work from those of painters but—as with Monet—the paintings are far more novel than art critics sometimes assert.

2. Complete the sentences with the information from the passage.

1) When his work attracted the harshest criticism, Cézanne _____ from the group and spent more of his time in Aix-en-Provence.

2) Cézanne was a slow worker, putting a great deal of thought into _____—as most painters do, but by him taken to heroic lengths.

3) For a similar purpose, parts of the wall behind and the sofa are given patches of lighter tone, though the sofa on the viewer's left practically _____ the tiling: there is no sense of depth here.

4) The flowers of the Chinese primrose are also circular, as is the right (to us) side of their enclosing pot— _____ from the ellipse we would expect.

5) A warning because Cézanne is prized for what he led to—short-lived movements, promotion by critics, galleries and dealers, and investment opportunities for the wealthy as the traditional old masters were increasingly _____.

3. Put the following sentences in the right order according to Cézanne's life experience.

A. So continued Cézanne's quiet existence, monastically devoted to paintings that continually disappointed him and which he often destroyed.

B. In this late work Cézanne has moved further to abstraction: simplified shapes, an only-hinted-at solidity, a thrusting energy to the rock forms, and the almost complete loss of the third dimension.

C. From 1872, however, under Pissarro's tutelage, Cézanne began to paint out of doors, and exhibited with the Impressionists in 1874 and 1877.

D. In his middle forties, Cézanne married Marie-Hortense Fiquet, his long-suffering model/mistress, and achieved financial independence when his father died a year later.

E. Cézanne was born in Aix-en-Provence on January 19, 1839, the son of a wealthy banker whose allowance enabled Cézanne to continue producing works that brought in no money or critical approval.

F. Following an exhibition arranged for him by the Parisian art dealer Ambroise Vollard in 1895, Cézanne became better known, and in 1904 his work featured in a major official exhibition.

G. The brush strokes are now laid like overlapping tiles, but the composition is conventional: three planes (trees, quarry wall and mountain), a rectilinear grid and a gentle swirling motion brought out by the rounded rock forms, the trees to the right and the shape of Mont Sainte Victoire.

(   ) —— (   ) —— (   ) —— (   ) —— (   ) —— (   ) —— (   )

 Language in Use

4 **Fill in the blanks with the words from the word bank. Make changes when necessary.**

comparative	isolate	represent	incomplete	mud
waver	cast	devote	ambiguous	warn

1) He quarreled bitterly with Zola in 1886 over the novelist's portrayal of a failed painter, becoming more socially _____ than ever.

2) Young artists traveled down to see him, and the last years to his death in Aix on October 22, 1906 were _____ happy.

3) Each brush stroke not only _____ "something" of what he saw, but also took account of all previous brushstrokes in aiming for two things.

4) The color scheme is triadic—secondary triadic, as the colors are not primary but in fact quite _____.

5) The curve of the bust, and the shadow it _____ give the sitter's torso some modeling.

6) In short, the rendering of the third dimension is only local, and this _____ effect creates an undulating surface not far detached from the canvas plane.

7) The sitter's head is left as an assembly of curved planes, which looks _____ finished or "knobby" by the earlier expectations of art.

8) The cloth and apples are _____ in the third dimension: receding comfortably into the distance in the left corner of the table.

9) It's Cézanne's intense _____ to his craft that distinguishes his work from those of followers, but—as with Monet—the paintings are far less novel than art critics sometimes assert.

10) Cézanne's art is an inspiration and a _____.

5 **Translate the following paragraph into Chinese.**

It's Cézanne's intense devotion to his craft that distinguishes his work from those of followers, but—as with Monet—the paintings are far less novel than art critics sometimes assert. Nonetheless, the very action of painting, the thought that goes into each and every brushstroke, became important for one line of development, that of abstract painting.

Oral Practice

6 **Read the passage again and discuss with your partner about the influence of Cézanne's painting. You may use the following terms in your discussion.**

the first rank	likeness	opportunities	abstract painting
investment	distinguish	a photographic	Cubism and Expressionism

Passage Two Painting Time: Impressionism and the Modern Temporal Order

1 It is often said that Impressionism sought to make represented time and the time of representation **coterminous**. With its seemingly quick and **unpolished** touch, it gave the modern cultures of speed their first appropriately modernist forms. But art historians have rarely if ever interrogated the concrete histories and technologies

coterminous *adj.* 相连的

unpolished *adj.* 未经润饰的

of time (and time keeping) that underwrote this **seismic** stylistic shift or to inquire into the links between quickening brushwork and the nineteenth century's industrialization of time. This is especially remarkable given the fact that two key scientific events in the measuring of modern time—the advent of quantifiable nervous reaction time in France around 1865 and the standardization of universal time in 1884—overlap so precisely with the history of Impressionism, its rise in the mid-1860s, and the turn toward **Postimpressionism** around the mid-1880s.

❷ I propose an intimate correlation between the new **subjectivizations** of Impressionist picture-making and the period's growing regulation of time. Impressionism evinced an acute awareness of the particularly modern pressures of time. It **chronicled** the constant shifts in weather, the seasons and time of day, while heroizing the new practices of leisure time, the "time-off" from work. Proposing that the flux of visual experience could be distilled into forms compatible with Western easel painting, it nonetheless portrayed a seeming urgency of execution and a **concomitant** disrespect for the protocols of pictorial finish. All these figurations of freedom from temporal and pictorial constraints seemed in clear contrast to the electro-technical world of the modern clock during the so-called Second Industrial Revolution— or "The Age of Synergy" as Václav Smil calls the decades after 1860—and its drive toward a global telegraphic connectivity and exchange of goods. The regulation of time had been a crucial component of the Industrial Revolution from its eighteenth-century origins, especially after scheduled trains started running in the 1820s, but never before had the demand for **temporal** precision been as pervasive a feature of modern culture as in the age of electricity and global wiring, travel and commerce, starting in the 1860s and 1870s.

❸ Impressionism's aesthetic play with the laws and markets of time became possible only at a moment in history when the precise marking of time itself fully regulated commodity form: marketed as a coordinated system first through pneumatic and later through

seismic *adj.* 地震的

Postimpressionism *n.* 后印象派

subjectivization *n.* 主观化

chronicle *v.* 记录；把······载入编年史

concomitant *adj.* 相伴的；共存的

temporal *adj.* 暂时的

electrically coordinated city-wide clocks (as sold, for instance, by the Parisian Compagnie Générale des Horloges Pneumatiques, which not only offered clocks but the continual upkeep of their precision as well). The style's fusion of paint and time could have the wider cultural **resonance** it eventually gained only once time itself became fully quantifiable and its visibility recognized as a scientific—and economic—fact of modern global life. Impressionism is one of the period's crucial aesthetic innovations born of the "product" time, deeply aware of time's new prominence in urban life and its public clocks, train schedules, and so forth. "Seven twenty-three! Only seven more minutes until soup would be served," claimed a character in Paul Alexis's novel *Madame Meuriot* (1891) as just one of the many seemingly gratuitous indications of temporal order that help structure a complicated plot of **adultery**.

resonance *n.* 共鸣；反响

adultery *n.* 通奸

④ Impressionism's relation to technology, science, industry, and modernity can be seen in its iconography—the representations of clocks in Edgar Degas's or Paul Cézanne's work or the trains that populate so many an Impressionist canvas—and in its representation of leisure and industry, with the factories in the modern **landscape** and the lives lived away from work amidst their growing presence, as is the theme of much crucial art historical investigation, from T. J. Clark's influential work on the period to more recent studies, such as James H. Rubin's inquiry into Impressionism's industrialized landscapes. But I am more interested in locating an economy of time in Impressionism on a stylistic level as well as on a semantic one, what I want to call Impressionism's "social forms": in its new logics of brushwork and composition, redefinitions of the standards of painting, and translations of modern experience, just as much as in its modern subject matter of industrialized culture.

landscape *n.* 形势

⑤ Specifically, what does our critical vocabulary of the movement's **embellishments** of time—speed of execution, **instantaneity**, **momentariness**, presentness, and so on—evoke historically? The language of Impressionism's early reception

embellishment *n.* 修饰
instantaneity *n.* 立即；瞬时性
momentariness *n.* 瞬时性

is filled with temporal metaphors that still require more careful unpacking as to the range of their sociocultural meanings: in 1883, Jules Laforgue called Impressionism painting "in fifteen minutes"; Félix Fénéon affirmed that it was "four o'clock" in Georges Seurat's *A Sunday Afternoon on the Island of La Grande Jatte*; and in 1876, the critic Arthur Baignères called Impressionism "a kind of telegraphic mechanism" that fixed impressions like "the letters of a dispatch on azure-colored paper." How did it come to pass that such chronometric coordinates became a central tool in the exegesis of early modernist painting even if they could not be fully confirmed visually? Why have they so often survived into our accounts of the movement as in such influential books as Richard Brettell's *Impression: Painting Quickly in France 1860–1890* (2000) or Virginia Spate's *Claude Monet: The Color of Time* (1992)?

exegesis *n.* 注释，解释

⑥ Impressionism emerged at the precise moment when the scientific measurement of the speed of sensory transmission, of "reaction time," became possible. Claude Monet's early, oft-considered unfinished and "failed" attempts at bringing Impressionism into the large-scale format of his *Déjeuner sur l'herbe* (c. 1865) can be seen in light of "psychometry's" proof that there was no instantaneity of nervous transmission. Auguste Renoir's and Monet's depictions of the bathing spot of La Grenouillère encapsulated precise meanings of the "now" at the time, and such modern temporal frames can be seen in dialogue with the painters' pictorial demands for a more "speedy" execution. One of the most popular and trendy leisure spots of the late Second Empire, La Grenouillère became the site of contestation over definitions of the "present" and the "now" as a unit in time and the possible temporal durée of a phenomenon like the ever-changing experience of modernity. The collapse of an Impressionist aesthetic into the Postimpressionist order and systematicity of pointillism in the mid-1880s occurs at precisely the advent of global standardized time, set at the Meridian conference in Washington in 1884 with representatives from most industrialized nations present including France. George Seurat and Paul Signac's pictorial world of the synchronized "dots" of color—a pictorial innovation we generally

sensory *adj.* 感觉的

encapsulate *v.* 概述

synchronized *adj.* 同步的

agree first emerged in 1885—was hardly conceivable outside the frame of the universal hour and its invisible if crucial regulation of a global system of temporal and spatial units.

7 My study of the history of Impressionism and the history of the period's construction of time engages in a new way the twinned aspirations of freedom from and fears of regulation so typical of the modern world—something that could stand as a metaphor of Impressionist picture-making itself. Impressionism's high-keyed temporal anxiety—its conflation of represented time, experienced time, and the time of representation—is one of the period's most sensitive **registrations** of industrial time's regulatory power.

registration *n.* 登记；记录

Extended Activities

Each of the following statements contains information given in one of the paragraphs in the passage. Identify the paragraph from which the information is derived and put the corresponding number in the space provided.

_____ 1) It recorded the change of time, while heroizing the new practices of leisure time, the "time-off" from work.

_____ 2) The language of Impressionism's early reception needs to be considered basing on the social background.

_____ 3) All these figurations of freedom from temporal and pictorial constraints showed contrast to the situation of the Second Industrial Revolution.

_____ 4) With its seemingly quick and unpolished touch, it promoted development of the modern cultures.

_____ 5) The style's fusion of paint and time would finally have the wider cultural resonance.

_____ 6) But I tend to have more interest in locating an economy of time in Impressionism on a stylistic level as well as on a semantic one.

_____ 7) How did it come to pass that such chronometric coordinates became a central tool in early modernist painting even if they could not actually be fully seen?

_____ 8) Impressionism's high-keyed temporal anxiety was a reflection of industrial time's regulatory power.

_____ 9) The transition of Impressionist aesthetic into the Postimpressionist order and systematicity of pointillism in the mid-1880s occurs at precisely the advent of global standardized time.

_____ 10) Impressionism emerged at the precise moment when there came into being the evaluation of sensory transmission and of "reaction time".

Answer the following questions based on the understanding of the passage.

1) When was the turn to Postimpressionism in history?

2) What is the relationship between the new subjectivizations of Impressionist picture-making and the period's growing regulation of time according to the writer?

3) How do we understand "Impressionism is one of the period's crucial aesthetic innovations born of the 'product' time" in Para. 3?

4) How is Impressionism's relation to technology, science, industry, and modernity shown?

5) What was the precise moment when Impressionism emerged?

Translate the following paragraph into English.

通常认为，印象主义应该实现作品表现的真实时间变化与创作时间的相互关联。印象主义以其似乎迅速且不加雕琢的笔触，第一次反映了急速变化的现代文化。但是艺术史家们很少或几乎没有关注这次剧烈的艺术转型背后的科技革命，或者是探究印象派迅速作画的特点与 19 世纪工业革命背景之间的关系。

Exploring

Work in groups to work out a simple appreciation report on a famous Impressionist painting. Your group work can be divided into the following steps.

Step 1   Find the painting your group is interested in.

Step 2   Search for background information about the painter and the painting. Discuss your feelings and opinions of it.

Step 3   Organize your ideas and give a presentation in class.

Mini-pedia

Impressionism

Impressionism is a style of painting that emerged in the mid- to late-1800s and emphasizes an artist's immediate *impression* of a moment or scene, usually communicated through the use of light and its reflection, short brushstrokes, and separation of colors. Impressionist painters often used modern life as their subject matter and painted quickly and freely.

Origins of the Term

Although some of the most respected artists of the Western canon were part of the Impressionist movement, the term "Impressionist" was originally intended as a derogatory term, used by art critics appalled at this style of painting.

In the mid-1800s, when the Impressionist movement was born, it was commonly accepted that "serious" artists blended their colors and minimized the appearance of brushstrokes to produce the "licked" surface preferred by the academic masters. Impressionism, in contrast, featured short, visible strokes—dots, commas, smears, and blobs.

One of Claude Monet's entries for the show, *Impression: Sunrise* (1873) was the first to inspire the critical nickname "Impressionism" in early reviews. To call someone an "Impressionist" in 1874 meant the painter had no skill and lacked the common sense to finish a painting before selling it.

The First Impressionist Exhibition

In 1874, a group of artists who dedicated themselves to this "messy" style pooled their resources to promote themselves in their own exhibition. The idea was radical. In those days, the French art world revolved around the annual Salon, an official exhibition sponsored by the French

government through its Académie des Beaux-Arts.

The group called themselves the Anonymous Society of Painters, Sculptors, Engravers, etc., and rented the photographer Nadar's studio in a new building, which was on its own a rather modern edifice. Their effort caused a brief sensation. For the average audience, the art looked strange, the exhibition space looked unconventional, and the decision to show their art outside of the Salon or the Academy's orbit (and even sell directly off the walls) seemed close to madness.

Indeed, these artists pushed the limits of art in the 1870s far beyond the range of "acceptable" practice.

Even in 1879, during the fourth Impressionist Exhibition, the French critic Henry Havard wrote: "I confess humbly I do not see nature as they do, never having seen these skies fluffy with pink cotton, these opaque and moiré waters, this multi-colored foliage. Maybe they do exist. I do not know them."

Impressionism and Modern Life

Impressionism created a new way of seeing the world. It was a way of seeing the city, the suburbs and the countryside as mirrors of the modernization that each of these artists perceived and wanted to record from his or her point of view. Modernity, as they knew it, became their subject matter. It replaced mythology, biblical scenes and historical events that dominated the revered "history" painting of their era.

In a sense, the spectacle of the street, cabaret or seaside resort became "history" painting for these stalwart Independents (also known as the Intransigents—the stubborn ones).

The Evolution of Postimpressionism

The Impressionists mounted eight shows from 1874 to 1886, although very few of the core artists exhibited in every show. After 1886, the gallery dealers organized solo exhibition or small group shows, and each artist concentrated on his or her own career.

Nevertheless, they remained friends (except for Degas, who stopped talking to Pissarro because he was an anti-Dreyfusard and Pissarro was Jewish). They stayed in touch and protected each other well into old age. Among the original group of 1874, Monet survived the longest. He died in 1926.

Some artists who exhibited with the Impressionists in the 1870s and 1880s pushed their art into different directions. They became known as Post-impressionists: Paul Cézanne, Paul Gauguin, and Georges Seurat, among others.

Reflection

Achievements	Yes	No
I am familiar with some basic facts of Impressionism.		
I have understood the artistic value and meaning of these works.		
I have learnt the way of looking into social background in appreciation of art works.		
I have acquired useful words and expressions related to painting.		

UNIT 4
EDUCATION

◇

GOALS

1 To become aware of the importance and impact of education;

2 To get to know the western educational concepts and systems;

3 To become aware of the differences between Chinese and western education;

4 To acquire some words and expressions about education.

Warming-up

Answer the following questions:

1. Why do people need education?
2. What do you know about western educational concepts?
3. What are the differences between Chinese and western educational systems?

Reading

Passage One On Education

By Albert Einstein

①   A day of celebration generally is in the first place dedicated to **retrospect**, especially to the memory of **personages** who have gained special distinction for the development of the cultural life. This friendly service for our **predecessors** must indeed not be neglected, particularly as such a memory of the best of the past is proper to stimulate the well-disposed of today to a courageous effort. But this should be done by someone who, from his youth, has been connected with this State and is familiar with its past, not by one who like a **gypsy** has wandered about and gathered his experiences in all kinds of countries.

②   Thus, there is nothing else left for me but to speak about such questions as, independently of space and time, always have been

retrospect n. 回顾，回想

personage n. 人；（尤指）要人，名人

predecessor n. 前任；前辈

gypsy n. 吉卜赛人

and will be connected with educational matters. In this attempt I cannot lay any claim to being an authority, especially as intelligent and well-meaning men of all times have dealt with educational problems and have certainly repeatedly expressed their views clearly about these matters. From what source shall I, as a partial layman in the realm of pedagogy, derive courage to **expound** opinions with no foundations except personal experience and personal conviction? If it were really a scientific matter, one would probably be tempted to silence by such considerations.

expound v. 解释，详细讲解

❸   However, with the affairs of active human beings it is different. Here knowledge of truth alone does not **suffice**; on the contrary, this knowledge must continually be renewed by ceaseless effort if it is not to be lost. It resembles a statue of marble, which stands in the desert, and is continuously threatened with burial by the shifting sand. The hands of service must ever be at work, in order that the marble continue lastingly to shine in the sun. To these serving hands mine also shall belong.

suffice v. 足够；有能力；满足……的需要；使满足

❹   The school has always been the most important means of transferring the wealth of tradition from one generation to the next. This applies today in an even higher degree than in former times, for through modern development of the economic life, the family as bearer of tradition and education has been weakened. The continuance and health of human society is therefore in a still higher degree dependent on the school than formerly.

❺   Sometimes one sees in the school simply the instrument for transferring a certain maximum quantity of knowledge to the growing generation. But that is not right. Knowledge is dead; the school, however, serves the living. It should develop in the young individuals those qualities and capabilities which are of value for the welfare of the commonwealth. But that does not mean that individuality should be destroyed and the individual become a mere tool of the community, like a bee or an ant. For a community of standardized individuals without personal **originality** and personal aims would be a poor community without possibilities

originality n. 独创性，创造性

for development. On the contrary, the aim must be the training of independently acting and thinking individuals, who, however, see in the service of the community their highest life problem. So far as I can judge, the English school system comes nearest to the realization of this ideal.

6 But how shall one try to attain this ideal? Should one perhaps try to realize this aim by **moralizing**? Not at all. Words are and remain an empty sound, and the road to **perdition** has ever been accompanied by lip service to an ideal. But personalities are not formed by what is heard and said, but by labor and activity.

moralize *v.* 论道德，说教

perdition *n.* 毁灭

7 The most important method of education accordingly always has consisted of that in which the pupil was urged to actual performance. This applies as well to the first attempts at writing of the primary boy as to the doctor's thesis on graduation from the university, or as to the mere memorizing of a poem, the writing of a composition, the interpretation, and translation of a text, the solving of a mathematical problem or the practice of physical sport.

8 But behind every achievement exists the motivation which is at the foundation of it and which in turn is strengthened and nourished by the accomplishment of the undertaking. Here there are the greatest differences and they are of greatest importance to the educational value of the school. The same work may owe its origin to fear and **compulsion**, ambitious desire for authority and distinction, or loving interest in the object and a desire for truth and understanding, and thus to that divine curiosity which every healthy child possesses, but which so often is weakened early. The educational influence, which is exercised upon the pupil by the accomplishment of one and the same work may be widely different, depending upon whether fear of hurt, **egoistic** passion, or desire for pleasure and satisfaction are at the bottom of this work. And nobody will maintain that the administration of the school and the attitude of the teachers do not have an influence upon the molding of the psychological foundation for pupils.

compulsion *n.* 强制，强迫

egoistic *adj.* 自我中心的，自私自利的

9   To me the worst thing seems to be for a school principally to work with methods of fear, force, and artificial authority. Such treatment destroys the sound sentiments, the sincerity, and the self-confidence of the pupil. It produces the **submissive** subject. It is comparatively simple to keep the school free from this worst of all evils. Give into the power of the teacher the fewest possible **coercive** measures, so that the only source of the pupil's respect for the teacher is the human and intellectual qualities of the latter.

submissive *adj.* 顺从的，唯命是从的

coercive *adj.* 强制的，强迫的；高压的

10   The second-named motive, ambition, or in milder terms, the aiming at recognition and consideration, lies firmly fixed in human nature. With absence of mental stimulus of this kind, human cooperation would be entirely impossible; the desire for the approval of one's fellow-man certainly is one of the most important binding powers of society. In this complex of feelings, constructive and destructive forces lie closely together. Desire for approval and recognition is a healthy motive; but the desire to be acknowledged as better, stronger, or more intelligent than a fellow being or fellow scholar easily leads to an excessively egoistic psychological adjustment, which may become **injurious** for the individual and for the community. Therefore, the school and the teacher must guard against employing the easy method of creating individual ambition, in order to induce the pupils to diligent work.

injurious *adj.* 伤害的；中伤的

11   Darwin's theory of the struggle for existence and the selectivity connected with it has by many people been cited as authorization of the encouragement of the spirit of competition. Some people also in such a way have tried to prove **pseudo**-scientifically the necessity of the destructive economic struggle of competition between individuals. But this is wrong, because man owes his strength in the struggle for existence to the fact that he is a socially living animal. As little as a battle between single ants of an ant hill is essential for survival, just so little is this the case with the individual members of a human community.

pseudo *adj.* 假的；虚伪的

12   Therefore, one should guard against **preaching** to the young man success in the customary sense as the aim of life. For a

preach *v.* 宣扬；说教，布道

successful man is he who receives a great deal from his fellowmen, usually incomparably more than corresponds to his service to them. The value of a man, however, should be seen in what he gives and not in what he is able to receive.

⑬ The most important motive for work in the school and in life is the pleasure in work, pleasure in its result, and the knowledge of the value of the result to the community. In the awakening and strengthening of these psychological forces in the young man, I see the most important task given by the school. Such a psychological foundation alone leads to a joyous desire for the highest possessions of men, knowledge and artist-like **workmanship**.

workmanship *n.* 技艺，工艺

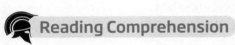

Reading Comprehension

1 **Decide whether the following statements are true or false. Write T for true and F for false.**

_____ 1) This friendly service for our predecessors should be done by someone like Albert Einstein who, from his youth, had been connected with this State and was familiar with its past.

_____ 2) Due to modern development of the economic life, the family as bearer of tradition and education has been weakened. So the continuance and health of human society is still largely dependent on the school.

_____ 3) A community of individuals with personal innovation and goals would have the huge potential for development.

_____ 4) The desire to be acknowledged as better, stronger or more intelligent than a fellow being or fellow scholar is beneficial to the individual and the community.

_____ 5) The value of a man should be shown in what he receives.

2 **Complete the sentences with the information from the passage.**

1) The knowledge of truth must continually be renewed by ceaseless effort. It is like a statue of marble in the desert. In order to make the marble continue lastingly to shine in the sun, the hands of service must ever be _____.

2) It is not right for one to see school as simply the _____ for _____ knowledge to the next generation.

3) The aim of school must be the training of _____ acting and thinking individuals. But, to realize this aim is not dependent on _____.

4) _____ applies to the primary boy's first attempts at writing, the doctor's _____ from the university, the mere _____ of a poem, the _____ of a text, the solving of a mathematical problem or the practice of physical sport.

5) Treating pupils with fear, force and artificial authority _____ their sound sentiments, the _____ and the _____.

In his speech about education, Albert Einstein clearly stated what he was for and what he was against. Read the passage again and make a list about them.

For	Against
1.	1.
2.	2.
3.	3.
4.	4.
5.	5.

Language in Use

Fill in the blanks with the words from the word bank. Make changes when necessary.

coercive	originality	compulsion	expound	suffice
moralize	predecessor	personage	egoistic	retrospect

1) In _____, I wish that I had thought about alternative courses of action.

2) There is no evidence for such a historical _____.

3) He's backing away from the policies and style of his _____.

4) The speaker has an hour to _____ his views to the public.

5) A cover letter should never exceed one page; often a far shorter letter will _____.

6) We must promote _____ and encourage innovation.

7) Some critics have complained that former President Obama offered little decisive action and _____ too much.

8) Many universities argued that students learned more when they were in classes out of choice rather than _____.

9) This ethical doctrine holds that people are basically selfish and _____.

10) The eighteenth-century Admiralty had few _____ powers over its officers.

 Translate the following paragraph into Chinese.

Sometimes one sees in the school simply the instrument for transferring a certain maximum quantity of knowledge to the growing generation. But that is not right. Knowledge is dead; the school, however, serves the living. It should develop in the young individuals those qualities and capabilities which are of value for the welfare of the commonwealth. But that does not mean that individuality should be destroyed and the individual become a mere tool of the community, like a bee or an ant. For a community of standardized individuals without personal originality and personal aims would be a poor community without possibilities for development. On the contrary, the aim must be the training of independently acting and thinking individuals, who, however, see in the service of the community their highest life problem.

 Oral Practice

 Read the passage again and discuss with your partner about the most impressive part of Albert Einstein's speech entitled *On Education*. You may use the following expressions in your discussion.

transfer	knowledge	individuals	pleasure	empty sound
school	individuality	community	originality	recognition
develop	moralizing	capabilities	independently	educational value
aim	intellectual	motivation	actual performance	

Passage Two Remarks of Former President Barack Obama

1 Over the last few weeks, I have been making the case that we need to act now on the American Jobs Act, so we can put folks back to work and start building an economy that lasts into the future.

2 Education is an essential part of this economic **agenda**. It is an undeniable fact that countries who out-educate us today will out-compete us tomorrow. Businesses will hire wherever the

agenda *n.* 议事日程

highly-skilled, highly-trained workers are located.

❸ But today, our students are **sliding** against their peers around the globe. Today, our kids **trail** too many other countries in math, science, and reading. As many as a quarter of our students aren't even finishing high school. And we have fallen to 16th in the proportion of our young people with a college degree, even though we know that sixty percent of new jobs in the coming decade will require more than a high school diploma.

slide *v.* 滑落；下跌；打滑；衰落（成）；逐渐降低
trail *v.*（在比赛等中）输；拖曳；拖沓而行；跟在……后面

❹ What this means is that if we're serious about building an economy that lasts—an economy in which hard work pays off with the opportunity for solid middle-class jobs—we had better be serious about education. We have to pick up our game and raise our standards.

❺ As a nation, we have an obligation to make sure that all children have the resources they need to learn—quality schools, good teachers, the latest textbooks and the right technology. That's why the jobs bill I sent to Congress would put tens of thousands of teachers back to work across the country, and modernize at least 35,000 schools. And Congress should pass that bill right now.

❻ But money alone won't solve our education problems. We also need reform. We need to make sure that every classroom is a place of high expectations and high performance.

❼ That's been our vision since **taking office**. And that's why instead of just pouring money into a system that's not working, we launched a competition called Race to the Top. To all fifty states, we said, "If you show us the most innovative plans to improve teacher quality and student achievement, we'll show you the money."

take office 就职；任职

❽ For less than one percent of what we spend on education each year, Race to the Top has led states across the country to raise their standards for teaching and learning. These standards were developed, not by Washington, but by Republican and Democratic governors throughout the country. And since then, we have seen what's possible when reform isn't just a top-down **mandate**, but the work of local teachers and principals; school boards and communities.

mandate *n.* 授权；命令；强制执行

9 That's why in my State of the Union address this year, I said that Congress should reform the No Child Left Behind law based on the same principles that have guided Race to the Top.

10 While the goals behind No Child Left Behind were **admirable**, experience has taught us that the law has some serious flaws that are hurting our children instead of helping them. Teachers are being forced to teach to a test, while subjects like history and science are being **squeezed out**. And in order to avoid having their schools labeled as failures, some states lowered their standards in a race to the bottom.

admirable *adj.* 令人钦佩的；极好的，绝妙的；值得赞扬的

squeeze out 挤出；排挤；榨出

11 These problems have been obvious to parents and educators all over this country for years. But for years, Congress has failed to fix them. So now, I will. Our kids only get one shot at a decent education. And they can't afford to wait any longer.

12 Yesterday, I announced that we'll be giving states more **flexibility** to meet high standards for teaching and learning. It's time for us to let states, schools and teachers come up with innovative ways to give our children the skills they need to compete for the jobs of the future.

flexibility *n.* 机动性，灵活性

13 This will make a huge difference in the lives of students all across the country. Yesterday, I was with Ricky Hall, the principal of a school in Worcester, Massachusetts. Every single student who graduated from Ricci's school in the last three years went on to college. But because they didn't meet the standards of No Child Left Behind, Ricci's school was labeled as failing last year.

14 That will change because of what we did yesterday. From now on, we'll be able to encourage the progress at schools like Ricci's. From now on, people like John Becker, who teaches at one of the highest-performing middle schools in D.C., will be able to focus on teaching his 4th graders math in a way that improves their performance instead of just teaching to a test. **Superintendents** like David Estrop from Ohio will be able to focus on improving teaching and learning in his district instead of spending all his time on **bureaucratic** mandates from Washington that don't get results.

superintendent *n.* 主管；监督人，管理人

bureaucratic *adj.* 官僚的，官僚主义的，官僚作风的

⓵⓹ This isn't just the right thing to do for our kids—it's the right thing to do for our country, and our future. It is time to put our teachers back on the job. It is time to rebuild and modernize our schools. And it is time to raise our standards, up our game, and do everything it takes to prepare our children to succeed in the global economy. Now is the time to once again make our education system the envy of the world.

⓵⓺ Thanks for listening.

Extended Activities

Each of the following statements contains information given in one of the paragraphs in the passage. Identify the paragraph from which the information is derived and put the corresponding number in the space provided.

_____ 1) It is time to rebuild and modernize American schools, to raise educational standards, to do everything it takes to prepare American children to succeed in the global economy.

_____ 2) It's time to give states more flexibility to let states, schools and teachers come up with innovative ways to improve teaching and students' learning.

_____ 3) Education plays an important role in the economy.

_____ 4) No Child Left Behind law shows some serious problems.

_____ 5) Race to the Top has led states across the country to raise teaching and learning standards which were developed by Republican and Democratic governors throughout the country.

_____ 6) Congress has failed to fix the education problems for years.

_____ 7) Race to the Top aims to find the most innovative plans which can improve teacher quality and student achievement.

_____ 8) Today's American students cannot compete with foreign peers in many fields.

_____ 9) We need money and reform to solve our education problems.

_____ 10) The Congress should pass the jobs bill right now because it would put tens of thousands of teachers back to work across the country, and modernize at least 35,000 schools.

Answer the following questions based on the understanding of the passage.

1) What is the American Jobs Act?

2) What is the current situation of American education?

3) What is the competition called Race to the Top?

4) What has Race to the Top achieved?

5) What are some serious problems about the No Child Left Behind law?

Translate the following paragraphs into English.

但是现在，我们学生的成绩与世界上的同龄孩子相比正在下滑。今天，我们的孩子们在数学、科学和阅读等方面已经落后于很多国家，其中有 1/4 的学生甚至连高中都没有毕业。年轻人中拥有大学学位的比例已经降至世界第 16 位，尽管我们知道未来十年里百分之六十的新工作要求的绝不仅仅是高中学历。

这意味着，如果我们真的想建设可持续的经济——这种只要努力工作就可以获得稳定的中产就业机会的经济——我们最好要认真对待教育。我们必须回到赛场，发挥我们的优势，提高我们的标准。

Exploring

Work in groups to make a presentation about the ideal education in your eyes. The following procedures are for your reference.

Step 1   Obtain some useful information related to education from the library and the Internet.

Step 2   Have a group discussion about the definition, characteristics and modes of the ideal education.

Step 3   Give a presentation and share what you know with the rest of the class.

Mini-pedia

Understanding the American Education System

The American education system offers a rich field of choices for international students. There is such an array of schools, programs and locations that the choices may overwhelm students, even those from the U.S. As you begin your school search, it's important to familiarize yourself with the American education system. Understanding the system will help you narrow your choices and develop your education plan.

Primary and Secondary Schools

Prior to higher education, American students attend primary and secondary schools for a combined total of 12 years. These years are referred to as the first through twelfth grades.

Around age six, U.S. children begin primary school, which is most commonly called "elementary school". They attend five or six years and then go onto secondary school.

Secondary school consists of two programs: the first is "middle school" or "junior high school" and the second program is "high school". A diploma or certificate is awarded upon graduation from high school. After graduating high school (12th grade), U.S. students may go on to college or university. College or university study is known as "higher education".

Grading System

Just like American students, you will have to submit your academic transcripts as part of your application for admission to university or college. Academic transcripts are official copies of your academic work. In the U.S. this includes your "grades" and "grade point average" (GPA), which are measurements of your academic achievement. Courses are commonly graded using percentages, which are converted into letter grades.

The U.S. Higher Education System: Levels of Study

• First Level: Undergraduate

A student, who is attending a college or university and has not earned a bachelor's degree, is studying at the undergraduate level. It typically takes about four years to earn a bachelor's degree. You can either begin your studies in pursuit of a bachelor's degree at a community college or a four-year university or college.

In your first two years of study, you will generally be required to take a wide variety of classes in different subjects, commonly known as prerequisite courses: literature, science, the social sciences, the arts, history, and so forth. This helps you achieve a general knowledge, a foundation, of a variety of subjects prior to focusing on a specific field of study.

Many students choose to study at a community college in order to complete the first two years of prerequisite courses. They will earn an Associate of Arts (AA) transfer degree and then transfer to a four-year university or college.

A "major" is the specific field of study in which your degree is focused. For example, if someone's major is journalism, they will earn a Bachelor of Arts in Journalism. You will be required to take a certain number of courses in this field in order to meet the degree requirements of your major. You must choose your major at the beginning of your third year of school.

A very unique characteristic of the American higher education system is that you can change your major multiple times if you choose. It is extremely common for American students to switch majors at some point in their undergraduate studies. Often, students discover a different field that they excel in or enjoy. The American education system is very flexible. Keep in mind though that switching majors may result in more courses, which means more time and money.

• Second Level: Graduate in Pursuit of a Master's Degree

Presently, a college or university graduate with a bachelor's degree may want to seriously think about graduate study in order to enter certain professions or advance their career. This degree is usually mandatory for higher-level positions in library science, engineering, behavioral health, education, etc.

A graduate program is usually a division of a university or college. To gain admission, you will need to take the GRE (Graduate Record Examination). Certain master's programs require specific tests, such as the LSAT for law school, the GRE or GMAT for business school, and the MCAT for medical school.

Graduate programs in pursuit of a master's degree typically take one to two years to complete. For example, the MBA (Master of Business Administration) is an extremely popular degree program that takes about two years. Other master's programs, such as journalism, only take one year.

The majority of a master's program is spent in classroom study and a graduate student must prepare a long research paper called a "master's thesis" or complete a "master's project."

•**Third Level: Graduate in Pursuit of a Doctorate Degree**

Many graduate schools consider the attainment of a master's degree the first step towards earning a PhD (doctorate). But at other schools, students may prepare directly for a doctorate without also earning a master's degree. It may take three years or more to earn a PhD degree. For international students, it may take as long as five or six years.

For the first two years of the program most doctoral candidates enroll in classes and seminars. At least another year is spent conducting first-hand research and writing a thesis or dissertation. This paper must contain views, designs, or research that has not been previously published.

A doctoral dissertation is a discussion and summary of the current scholarship on a given topic. Most U.S. universities awarding doctorates also require their candidates to have a reading knowledge of two foreign languages, to spend a required length of time "in residence", to pass a qualifying examination that officially admits candidates to the PhD program, and to pass an oral examination on the same topic as the dissertation.

Reflection

Achievements	Yes	No
I am aware of the importance and impact of education.		
I have understood the western educational concepts and system.		
I am aware of the differences between Chinese and western education.		
I have acquired some useful words and expressions related to education.		

UNIT 5
LITERATURE

◆

GOALS

1 To know the different genres of western literature;

2 To become aware of the principles of British poetry;

3 To familiarize with some famous writers and poets in western literature.

Warming-up

Match the masterpieces with the writers respectively.

Hamlet	Charles Dickens
Pride and Prejudice	Mark Twain
A Tale of Two Cities	George Bernard Shaw
The Adventures of Tom Sawyer	Jane Austen
Pygmalion	William Shakespeare

Reading

Passage One William Butler Yeats

❶ Very early, in the first bloom of youth, William Butler Yeats emerged as a poet with an indisputable right to the name; his autobiography shows that the inner promptings of the poet determined his relations to the world even when he was a mere boy.

❷ He was born in an artistic home—in Dublin—thus beauty naturally became a vital necessity for him. He showed artistic powers, and his education was devoted to the satisfying of this tendency; little effort was made to **secure** traditional schooling. He was educated for the most part in England, his second fatherland; nonetheless, his decisive development was linked to Ireland, chiefly to the comparatively unspoiled **Celtic** district of Connaught where his family had their summer home. There he **inhaled** the

secure *v.* 使安全；获得

Celtic *adj.* 凯尔特人的
inhale *v.* 吸入

imaginative mysticism of popular belief and popular stories which is the most distinctive feature of his people, and amidst a primitive nature of mountain and sea he became absorbed in a passionate endeavor to capture its very soul.

❸　However, he abandoned his training in the fine arts soon after he had grown up in order to devote himself to poetry, for which his **inclination** was strongest. But this training is evident throughout his whole career, both in the intensity with which he worships form and personal style and, still more, in the **paradoxically audacious** solution of problems in which his **acute** but fragmentary philosophical speculation sought its way to what he needed for his own peculiar nature.

inclination *n.* 爱好；倾向

paradoxically *adv.* 自相矛盾地

audacious *adj.* 无畏的

acute *adj.* 敏锐的

❹　The literary world he entered, when he settled down in London at the end of the 1880s, did not offer him much positively, but it at least offered him fellowship in opposition, which to **pugnacious** youth seems particularly dear. It was filled with weariness and rebellion toward the spirit of the times which had prevailed just before, namely that of **dogmatic** natural science and naturalistic art. There were few whose hostility was so deeply grounded as that of Yeats, altogether intuitive, visionary, and **indomitably** spiritualistic as he was.

pugnacious *adj.* 好斗的

dogmatic *adj.* 教条的

indomitably *adv.* 不屈服地

❺　He was disturbed not only by the **cocksureness** of natural science and the narrowness of reality-aping art; even more, he was horrified by the **dissolution** of personality and the **frigidity** which issued from skepticism, by the **desiccation** of imagination and emotional life. Events proved him to be terribly right. Even more beautiful kinds of social utopianism, represented by the greatly admired poet William Morris, did not **captivate** such an individualist as young Yeats. Later he found his way to the people, and then not as an abstract conception, but as the Irish people, to whom he had been close as a child. What he sought in that people was not the masses stirred by present day demands, but a historically developed soul which he wished to arouse to more conscious life.

cocksureness *n.* 过于自信

dissolution *n.* 消亡

frigidity *n.* 冷淡

desiccation *n.* 干枯

captivate *v.* 迷惑；迷住

6   In the intellectual unrest of London, things nationally Irish remained dear to Yeats' heart; this feeling was nurtured by summer visits to his homeland and by comprehensive studies of its **folklore** and customs. His earlier lyrics are almost exclusively built on his impressions from these. His early poems immediately won high **esteem** in England because the new material, with its strong appeal to the imagination, received a form which, despite its special characteristics, was nevertheless linked closely with several of the noblest traditions of English poetry. The blending together of Celtic and English, which had never been successfully effected in the political **sphere**, became a reality here in the world of poetic imagination—a symptom of no small spiritual significance.

folklore *n.* 民俗

esteem *n.* 尊重

sphere *n.* 范围

7   However much Yeats had read of English masters, his verse has a new character. The **cadence** and the colors have changed, as if they had been moved to another air—that of the Celtic twilight by the sea. There is a greater element of song than is usual in modern English poetry. The music is more **melancholy**, and, under the gentle rhythm, which for all its freedom moves as securely as a sleepwalker, we have a hint of yet another rhythm with the slow breathing of the wind and the eternal pulse of the powers of nature. When this art reaches its highest level it is absolutely magical, but it is seldom easy to grasp. It is indeed often so **obscure** that an effort is needed to understand it. This obscurity lies partly in the mysticism of the actual subject, but perhaps just as much in the Celtic **temperament**, which seems to be more distinguished by fire, delicacy, and **penetration** than by clearness.

cadence *n.* 韵律

melancholy *adj.* 忧郁的

obscure *adj.* 模糊的

temperament *n.* 气质
penetration *n.* 渗透；洞察力

8   Yeats' association with the life of a people saved him from the **barrenness**. Around him as the central point and leader arose, within a group of his countrymen in the literary world of London, that mighty movement which has been named the Celtic Revival and which created a new national literature, an Anglo-Irish literature.

barrenness *n.* 荒芜

9   The foremost and most **versatile** poet of this group was

versatile *adj.* 多才多艺的

Yeats. His **rousing** and **rallying** personality caused the movement to grow and flower very quickly, by giving a common aim to **hitherto scattered** forces or by encouraging new forces previously unconscious of their existence.

rousing *adj.* 活泼的；充满活力的

rally *v.* 集合；团结

hitherto *adv.* 迄今

scattered *adj.* 分散的

⑩ In his plays as well as in his clearest and most beautiful lyrics, Yeats has achieved what few poets have been able to do: he has succeeded in preserving contact with his people while upholding the most aristocratic artistry. His poetical work has arisen in an exclusively artistic milieu which has had many **perils**; but without **abjuring** the articles of his aesthetic faith, his burning and questing personality has **contrived** to keep itself free from aesthetic emptiness. He has been able to follow the spirit that early appointed him the interpreter of his country, a country that had long waited for someone to **bestow** on it a voice. It is not too much to call such a life's work great.

peril *n.* 危险

abjure *v.* 避免；公开放弃

contrive *v.* 设法做到

bestow *v.* 授予；放置

 **Reading Comprehension**

Decide whether the following statements are true or false. Write **T** for true and **F** for false.

_____ 1) Yeats was educated for the most part in Ireland so that he was heavily influenced by the Celtic culture.

_____ 2) Yeats did not learn fine arts any more because of his strongest inclination in poetry.

_____ 3) When Yeats went to London, he was greatly attracted to the atmosphere in the literature world of London.

_____ 4) Yeats' connection with the Irish people empowered him.

_____ 5) Yeats' verse was fresh even though he had read many English masters.

Each of the following statements contains information given in one of the paragraphs in the passage. Identify the paragraph from which the information is derived and put the corresponding number in the space provided.

_____ 1) Yeats' rousing and rallying personality caused the movement to grow and flower very quickly.

_____ 2) Yeats took in the imaginative mysticism which is the most distinctive feature of his people, and amidst a primitive nature of mountain and sea he became absorbed in a passionate endeavor to capture its very soul.

_____ 3) Yeats was nurtured by summer visits to his homeland and its folklore and customs, and Irish spirits remained dear to him.

_____ 4) Without abjuring the articles of his aesthetic faith, his burning and questing personality has contrived to keep itself free from aesthetic emptiness.

_____ 5) Even more beautiful kinds of social utopianism, represented by the greatly admired poet William Morris, did not captivate such an individualist as young Yeats. Later he found his way to the people.

_____ 6) The music of Yeats is more melancholy, and, under the gentle rhythm, we have a hint of yet another rhythm with the slow breathing of the wind and the eternal pulse of the powers of nature.

Fill in the following table with the information from the passage.

Paras.	Main Ideas	Supporting Details
1–3	Yeats was interested in poetry and devoted himself to it.	• Early years: He showed 1) _____ powers, and his education was devoted to the satisfying of this tendency. He was educated for the most part in 2) _____, his second fatherland; nonetheless his 3) _____ development was linked to 4) _____. • However, he 5) _____ his training in the 6) _____ soon after he had 7) _____ in order to devote himself to poetry.
4–5	The literary world in London did not offer him much 8)_____, but his fellowship in 9)_____.	• He was tired of and rebelled against the 10) _____ natural science and 11) _____ art. • He was horrified by the 12) _____ of personality and the 13) _____ which issued from 14) _____ by the 15) _____ of imagination and emotional life.

Paras.	Main Ideas	Supporting Details
6–7	Yeats' fresh literary features came from his understanding of Irish people.	• He was 16) _____ by summer visits to his homeland and by comprehensive studies of its 17) _____ and 18) _____. • The 19) _____ together of Celtic and English became a reality here in the world of poetic imagination—a symptom of no small 20) _____ significance. • However much Yeats had read of 21) _____ masters, his verse has a 22) _____ character: There is a 23) _____ element of song than is usual in modern English poetry. The music is more 24) _____. The 25) _____ of his poems lies partly in the mysticism of the actual subject, but perhaps just as much in the Celtic 26) _____, which seems to be more distinguished by fire, delicacy, and 27) _____ than by 28) _____.
8–10	Yeats' association with the life of a people saved him from the 29) _____.	• The mighty movement which has been named the 30) _____ arose around him, and a new national literature, an 31) _____ literature, was created. • His 32) _____ and 33) _____ personality caused the movement to 34) _____ and 35) _____ very quickly. • He has been able to 36) _____ the spirit that early appointed him the 37) _____ of his country, a country that had long waited for someone to 38) _____ on it a 39) _____.

Language in Use

Fill in the blanks with the words from the word bank. Make changes when necessary.

inhale	inclination	acute	obscure	melancholy
penetration	scatter	contrive	peril	dissolution

1) As you _____, breathe energy up from the Earth, through your legs, and up through the rest of your body.

2) He stayed on until the _____ of the firm in 1948.

3) When she lost her sight, her other senses grew more _____.

4) You always follow your own _____ instead of considering other people's feelings.

5) The contracts are written in _____ language.

6) The only sounds were the distant, _____ cries of the seagulls.

7) Tomorrow there will be a few _____ showers.

8) She didn't speak any English, but we _____ to communicate using sign language.

9) Her mother had warned her about the _____ of living alone.

10) Explorers _____ into unknown regions.

 **Translate the following paragraph into Chinese.**

When this art reaches its highest level it is absolutely magical, but it is seldom easy to grasp. It is indeed often so obscure that an effort is needed to understand it. This obscurity lies partly in the mysticism of the actual subject, but perhaps just as much in the Celtic temperament, which seems to be more distinguished by fire, delicacy, and penetration than by clearness.

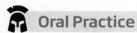 **Oral Practice**

Read the passage again and retell it. The following four parts should be included in your retelling.

- Yeats' life experience
- The influence of the literary world in London on Yeats
- Yeats' association with Irish people
- Yeats' new artistic features

Passage Two **Poems**

Sonnet 18

William Shakespeare

Shall I compare thee to a summer's day?

Thou art more lovely and more **temperate**:

Thou art: You are

temperate *adj.* 温和的

Rough winds do shake the darling buds of May,

And summer's **lease** hath all too short a date:　　　　　　lease *n.* 时期

Sometimes too hot the eye of heaven shines

And often is his gold complexion **dimmed**;　　　　　　dimmed *adj.* 暗淡的

And every fair from fair sometimes declines,

By chance or nature's changing course **untrimmed**;　　　untrimmed *adj.* 未装饰的

But **thy** eternal summer shall not fade,　　　　　　　　thy: your

Nor lose possession of that fair thou **ow'st**;　　　　　　ow'st: own

Nor shall death brag thou wander'st in his shade,

When in eternal lines to time thou **grow'st**:　　　　　　grow'st: grow

So long as men can breathe, or eyes can see,

So long lives this, and this gives life to **thee**.　　　　　thee: you

I Wandered Lonely as a Cloud

William Wordsworth

I wandered lonely as a cloud

That floats on high **o'er vales** and hills,　　　　　　　o'er: over

When all at once I saw a crowd,　　　　　　　　　　　vales: valley 山谷

A host, of golden **daffodils**;　　　　　　　　　　　　daffodil *n.* 水仙花

Beside the lake, beneath the trees,

Fluttering and dancing in the breeze.

Continuous as the stars that shine

And twinkle on the milky way,

They stretched in never-ending line

Along the margin of a bay:

Ten thousand saw I at a glance,

Tossing their heads in **sprightly** dance.　　　　　　　sprightly *adj.* 活泼的

The waves beside them danced; but they

Outdid the sparkling waves in **glee**,　　　　　　　　　glee *n.* 快乐

A poet could not but be **gay**,　　　　　　　　　　　　gay *adj.* 快乐的

In such a jocund company;

I gazed—and gazed—but little thought

What wealth the show to me had brought:

For **oft**, when on my couch I lie
In **vacant** or in **pensive** mood,
They flash upon that inward eye
Which is the bliss of solitude;
And then my heart with pleasure fills,
And dances with the daffodils.

oft: often 常常

vacant *adj.* 空虚的

pensive *adj.* 悲伤的

 Extended Activities

1. Shakespeare writes his sonnets in the popular English poetry form of three quatrains and a couplet, which was first fully developed by Surrey. The sonnets mostly follow this form, although sometimes Shakespeare makes variations. You may find that the couplet is usually related to one of the general themes of the series, while the poets show their intelligence in creating the quatrains. In Sonnet 18, can you figure out what are the quatrains and what is the couplet? What are they? And how do they rhyme? Write down the metrical pattern.

2. Iambic tetrameter (抑扬格四音步) is a meter in poetry. It refers to a line consisting of four iambic feet. The word "tetrameter" simply means that there are four feet in the line; iambic tetrameter is a line comprising four iambs. Read *I Wandered Lonely as a Cloud* and pay attention to the iambs. Besides, the poem also follows a certain metrical pattern. Please write it down.

3. Answer the following questions based on the understanding of the two poems.

    1) What are the images you can find in these two poems, and what do they symbolize respectively?

    2) What are the themes of the two poems?

    3) In *Sonnet 18*, whom does the poet speak to? What is the message the poet proposes? What are the arguments? What is the conclusion?

    4) In *I Wandered Lonely as a Cloud*, why does the poet combine the use of present tense and past tense? How does it help with the theme?

Exploring

Recommend a novel or a poem in western literature to your partner. Your recommendation should include the following aspects:

- The background of the writer.
- A brief summary of the literary work.
- The reason why you recommend it.

Mini-pedia

William Shakespeare

William Shakespeare (26 April 1564—23 April 1616) was an English poet, playwright and actor, widely regarded as the greatest writer in the English language and the world's pre-eminent dramatist. He is often called England's national poet and the "Bard of Avon". His extant works, including collaborations, consist of approximately 39 plays, 154 sonnets, two long narrative poems and a few other verses, some of uncertain authorship. His plays have been translated into every major living language and are performed more often than those of any other playwright.

Shakespeare was born and brought up in Stratford-upon-Avon, Warwickshire. At the age of 18, he married Anne Hathaway, with whom he had three children: Susanna and twins Hamnet and Judith. Sometime between 1585 and 1592, he began a successful career in London as an actor, writer, and part-owner of a playing company called the Lord Chamberlain's Men, later known as the King's Men. At age 49 around 1613, he appears to have retired to Stratford, where he died three years later. Few records of

Shakespeare's private life survive, which has stimulated considerable speculation about such matters as his physical appearance, sexuality, religious beliefs and whether the works attributed to him were written by others.

 # Reflection

Achievements	Yes	No
I am familiar with the different genres of western literature.		
I have understood the principles of British poetry.		
I am familiar with some famous writers and poets in western literature.		

UNIT 6
FESTIVALS

◈

GOALS

1 To describe ways of celebrating holidays and festivals;

2 To get to know that ways to celebrate holidays may change with time;

3 To explore the significance of western festivals from the perspective of how people celebrate them;

4 To acquire some expressions related to holidays.

Warming-up

Answer the following questions:

1. Can you name some popular western holidays and festivals?
2. How do people celebrate western festivals in China?
3. Do you think holidays are always celebrated in the same ways regardless of the time and location?

Reading

Passage One The Evolution of the Holiday Celebration

By Stephen Nissenbaum

① For most Americans, Christmas is the most important holiday of the year.

② Yet that is largely an accident, **stemming from** a series of improbable changes **spanning** two millennia. A similar set of changes has affected the development of other seasonal holidays, like Hanukkah.

stem from 起源于
span v. 持续

③ Early Christians did not celebrate the **Nativity**. Christianity had been around for more than 350 years before the **church fathers** in Rome decided to add that event to the Christian calendar. They did so in part because many Christians were arguing that Jesus had not been an actual human being but rather a divine spirit—a

Nativity n. 耶稣的诞生
church father 教父

belief the church fathers considered **heretical**. What better way to **convince** Christians that Jesus was human than to **commemorate** his physical birth? The problem was that there was no evidence of when Jesus' birth took place. (Neither Luke nor Matthew, the two **gospel** writers who included stories of Jesus' Nativity in their narratives, had indicated the date, or even the season, of the event.)

4 The church fathers decided to place the new holiday in late December, virtually guaranteeing that it would be widely adopted because this was already a season of mid-winter **revels**, a **holdover** from **pagan** times. For the inhabitants of the Roman Empire, the holiday was called **Saturnalia**. This festival, which concluded on Dec. 23, was partly a holiday of lights that celebrated the winter **solstice**. But Saturn was the god of agricultural **abundance**, so his festival also marked the **bounty** of the completed harvest. Finally, the Saturnalia was a time of role **reversals** and seasonal license. Everyone took time off from ordinary labor. Slaves were granted temporary freedom and were treated by their masters to **lavish** banquets. The holiday was observed with feasting, drinking, gambling, etc.

5 As the church fathers hoped, Christmas became an important holiday. But by placing it at such a time, they all but gave up the ability to define it as a purely religious one: Christmas was not easy to Christianize. In fact, the festivities that for centuries would mark its celebration resembled those of Saturnalia and other mid-winter rituals. In England, bands of young men **roamed** from house to house, singing as they begged for alcohol and money. Later, in the American South, slaves were occasionally granted temporary freedom, encouraged to get drunk and, yes, treated by their masters to lavish banquets. All that helps explain why, as a consequence of the **Protestant** Reformation of the 1500s, **Puritans** in both Old and New England tried to **suppress** Christmas as a **vestige** of **paganism**. From 1659 to 1682 it was actually illegal to celebrate the holiday in Massachusetts.

heretical *adj.* 异端的；异教的
convince *v.* 说服；使确信
commemorate *v.* 庆祝；纪念

gospel *adj.* 传播福音的

revel *n.* 狂欢
holdover *n.* 剩余物；遗留影响
pagan *n.* 异教徒；无宗教信仰者
Saturnalia *n.* (古罗马) 农神节
solstice *n.* 至日
abundance *n.* 丰富
bounty *n.* 慷慨；丰富
reversal *n.* 逆转
lavish *adj.* 丰富的；浪费的

roam *v.* 漫游，漫步；流浪

Protestant *n.* 新教徒
Puritan *n.* 清教徒
suppress *v.* 废止
vestige *n.* 残余
paganism *n.* 异教；异教信仰

⑥ In the 1800s, Christmas was transformed into the familiar domestic and child-centered ritual it remains to this day, centered on the magical figure of Santa Claus. The transformation was both marked and **abetted** by the 1823 publication of Clement Clarke Moore's poem "A Visit from St. Nicholas" and, two decades later, by the **proliferation** of Christmas trees in the United States. At the same time, Christmas also became a commercial holiday. Even before 1830, shopkeepers were using Santa Claus to **tout** their wares, and the first Christmas-tree **vendors** appeared in the streets during the 1840s. Indeed, from the very beginning, the family-focused Christmas and the commercial Christmas have worked **in tandem** to **reinforce** each other.

abet *v.* 支持

proliferation *n.* 扩散

tout *v.* 兜售
vendor *n.* 卖主；小贩

in tandem 一前一后地；协力地

reinforce *v.* 加强，加固；强化

⑦ Vestiges of the older mid-winter traditions remain. Christmas lights, **wassail** songs and **mistletoe hark back to** those traditions. (So, in a way, does the occasional presence of the "naughty" Santa.) Then there are the office Christmas parties, with their **whiff** of alcohol and **flirtation**. And what about New Year's Eve, to which the **boisterous** old-time Christmas revels have been mostly **relegated**?

wassail *n.* 酒宴
mistletoe *n.* 槲寄生（圣诞节在室内悬挂的一种植物）
hark back to 使想起；和……相似
whiff *n.* 吸气或吹气
flirtation *n.* 调情
boisterous *adj.* 喧闹的
relegate *v.* 归入

⑧ The newer as well as the older Christmas practices involve powerful traditions of excess, when people **flout** the rules of ordinary behavior with **impunity**. In the old days, that violation often involved great feasting and drinking, **bawdy** revels and the reversal of social roles. Nowadays, it involves **excessive** spending—for presents that are almost by definition luxuries rather than necessities.

flout *v.* 嘲笑；藐视
impunity *n.* 不受惩罚
bawdy *adj.* 猥亵的，下流的

excessive *adj.* 过多的

⑨ Other competing, mid-winter traditions mirror those of the Christian holiday, and those traditions, too, have been changed by a series of historical accidents. Take the Jewish holiday of Hanukkah, the Jewish Festival of Lights, as an example.

⑩ Hanukkah originated nearly six centuries before Christmas as the celebration of a Hebrew military victory, the liberation of **Jerusalem** from its **Macedonian-Greek** occupiers. The story

Jerusalem *n.* 耶路撒冷（巴勒斯坦中部城市）
Macedonian-Greek 马其顿 – 希腊

of the miracle of lights—the **meager** quantity of oil that burned for eight days to **cleanse** the **profaned** temple—emerged as the central meaning of the holiday only 400 years afterward, after a subsequent (and unsuccessful) **revolt** against the Romans, probably because by then the Jewish leadership did not wish to draw attention to that successful earlier revolt against another occupying nation.

meager *adj.* 贫乏的

cleanse *v.* 净化

profane *v.* 亵渎

revolt *n.* 反抗

⑪   As Hanukkah was transformed into a festival of lights, commemorated by the nine-candled **menorah**, it, too, came to take on seasonal associations. The Jewish Talmud itself hints at linking Hanukkah not only to the winter solstice but also—like Christmas—to the completion of the harvest. (Not surprisingly, in the modern state of Israel the original military victory has reemerged as a central element of the Hanukkah story.)

menorah *n.* 多连灯烛台（犹太宗教仪式所用的一种烛台）

⑫   In recent times, Hanukkah, too, has largely become a child's holiday. Many Jewish parents give their children seasonal presents as abundant—and expensive—as those received by their Christian neighbors.

⑬   And with Hanukkah as with Christmas, a vestige remains of older mid-winter festivals. This is the **Dreidel**, a four-sided top that resembles the familiar six-sided **dice** and is used in similar fashion to determine how much money (or Hanukkah "gelt") the player receives—or owes. Thus Hanukkah, originating as the celebration of a military victory, now incorporates a host of other rituals: the commemoration of a divine miracle, a seasonal celebration of light and harvest, a focus on children and even a hint of mid-winter revelry.

Dreidel *n.* 四面陀螺（犹太人游戏所用）

dice *n.* 骰子

⑭   Over the centuries, through all those historical accidents, Hanukkah and Christmas have come to look a lot like each other.

Reading Comprehension

① Decide whether the following statements are true or false or not given. Write T for true, F for false and NG for not given.

_____ 1) Church fathers decided to celebrate Jesus' birthday on Dec. 23rd to make people believe that Jesus was a real human.

_____ 2) Christmas resembled Saturnalia in the ways how people celebrated it.

_____ 3) In England, Christmas was celebrated legally, while in the U.S., the celebration was illegal in the 1500s.

_____ 4) Christmas became a family holiday because of the increase in Christmas trees and Christmas tree vending.

_____ 5) Both the old and the new Christmas traditions can be featured as "over consumption".

② Answer the following questions with the understanding of the passage.

1) Why did Jews first celebrate Hanukkah?

2) When Hanukkah was transformed into a festival of lights, what did Jews associate it with?

3) Who gives gifts to children in recent years in Hanukkah? And what kind of gifts do children receive?

4) Despite the change in Hanukkah, what still remains as a game on the holiday?

5) What kind of festival is Hanukkah now?

③ Put the following sentences in the right order according to the sequence of the information in the passage.

A. As time goes on, the two holidays resemble each other a lot.

B. Hanukkah has now become a children's holiday, in which they receive gifts from family and neighbors.

C. Hanukkah was first celebrated in honor of the liberation of Jerusalem from its occupiers.

D. Similar to Christmas, Hanukkah has also changed throughout history.

E. People spent and consumed too much on Christmas in the past, and it is the same now.

F. Nativity, the birthday of Jesus, was not celebrated.

G. Christmas was first a religious holiday, but gradually it turned into a family holiday as well as a commercial day.

H. Transformed into a festival of lights, Hanukkah became a seasonal holiday.

I. Both Christmas and Hanukkah have experienced great changes over the years.

J. Church fathers decided to commemorate Jesus' birthday because they wanted to convince people that he was a human.

(   ) —— (   ) —— (   ) —— (   ) —— (   ) —— (   ) —— (   ) ——
(   ) —— (   ) —— (   )

Language in Use

Fill in each blank with the correct form of the word provided in the brackets.

1) She used to be terribly shy, but a year abroad have completely _____ her. (transformation)

2) The first music _____ machines that will allow people to buy and download songs in the street, at railway stations or in the pub are to be unveiled this week. (vendor)

3) Beware of Internet friends who make a habit of _____, persuasive lines and promises. (convince)

4) Such countries must have a higher dependence on foreign trade than those which contain natural resources in greater _____ and variety within their borders. (abundant)

5) When darkness fell that day, firecrackers began to pop, first sporadically, then bursting all over the _____. (neighbour)

6) I feel strange in the _____ of strangers. (present)

7) The Catholic _____ does not bind us to confess our sins indiscriminately to everybody. (religious)

8) A _____ stamp issued by China's postal service that represents this ancient cypress, shaped like a dragon intending to fly, is one much sought after among philatelists. (commemorate)

9) Not _____, the results showed that men and women found happiness in different ways. (surprise)

10) But many of the _____ of Christmas do not have anything to do with religion. (festivity)

Translate the following paragraph into Chinese.

In the 1800s, Christmas was transformed into the familiar domestic and child-centered ritual it remains to this day, centered on the magical figure of Santa Claus. The transformation was both marked and abetted by the 1823 publication of Clement Clarke Moore's poem "A Visit from St. Nicholas" and, two decades later, by the proliferation of Christmas trees in the United States. At the same time, Christmas also became a commercial holiday. Even before 1830, shopkeepers were using Santa Claus to tout their wares, and the first Christmas-tree vendors appeared in the streets during the 1840s. Indeed, from the very beginning, the family-focused Christmas and the commercial Christmas have worked in tandem to reinforce each other.

 Oral Practice

6 **Read the passage again. Make a comparison and talk about the similarities and differences between Christmas and the Jewish holiday of Hanukkah. You may use the following words and expressions in your discussion.**

birthday	Jesus	church fathers	commercial holiday
celebration	religious	domestic ritual	festival of lights
Jewish	military		

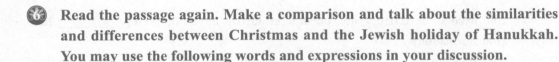 **Passage Two** Boxing Day—The Day After Christmas!

1 The first thing to say about Boxing Day is that its origins have nothing to do with boxing, or with putting used wrapping paper into boxes, or with boxing up all your unwanted presents, or indeed with football, horse racing, hunting, shopping, going for icy mass swims in the sea, or any of the other activities that now characterise the day after Christmas and act as an **antidote** to the **languor** that descends on households at around teatime on Christmas Day. The origins of Boxing Day lie not in sport, but in small acts of kindness.

antidote *n.* 解药
languor *n.* 倦怠

2 It is generally accepted that the name **derives from** the giving of Christmas "boxes", but the precise nature of those boxes and when they were first **dispensed** is disputed. One school of thought argues that the tradition began in churches in the Middle Ages.

derive from 源出，来自

dispense *v.* 分发

Parishioners collected money for the poor in **alms** boxes, and these were opened on the day after Christmas in honour of St. Stephen, the first Christian **martyr**, whose **feast day** falls on 26 December.

alms *n.* 施舍

martyr *n.* 殉道者；烈士
feast day 斋日；宗教节日

③   Some suggest the tradition is even older than that, dating back to the Christianised late Roman Empire, when similar collections were supposedly made for the poor in honour of St. Stephen, but the evidence is **sketchy**. All we can say for certain is that at some point St. Stephen's Day became associated with public acts of **charity**.

sketchy *adj.* 概略的

charity *n.* 慈善

④   It was no accident that Good King Wenceslas, who was actually a Duke of Bohemia in the 10th century, risked life and **limb** on a freezing winter night to feed some wretched peasant who had chosen a most **inclement** evening to gather winter fuel. His fabled act of generosity took place on the Feast of Stephen, on which day it was a Christian's duty to help those less fortunate than oneself. Or, as the somewhat laboured words of the **hymn** have it: "Therefore Christian men be sure, / Wealth or Rank possessing, / Ye who now will bless the poor / Shall yourselves find blessing."

limb *n.* 肢，臂
inclement *adj.* 狂风暴雨的

hymn *n.* 赞美诗；圣歌

⑤   The problem in terms of dating when the Feast of Stephen became the day for alms-giving and box-opening is that the Good King Wenceslas hymn, which was written by John Mason Neale, dates from 1853. As with most things to do with Christmas, it was the Victorians who **fleshed out** the meaning of Boxing Day. The Oxford English Dictionary dates the term to the 1830s. Neale clearly recognised the association of the day in the public mind with charity, and in 1871 St. Stephen's Day was **designated** a bank holiday. What had previously been an **amorphous** tradition now, thanks to the structured minds and myth-making tendencies of the Victorians, became a seasonal necessity.

flesh out 充实，具体化

designate *v.* 指定
amorphous *adj.* 无定形的

⑥   As part of this seasonal **beneficence**, some employers in the Victorian period gave Christmas boxes to their staff. In large households, after serving their employers on Christmas Day, domestic staff were allowed time off on Boxing Day to visit their

beneficence *n.* 慈善，善行；捐款

own families, and went off **clutching** Christmas boxes full of leftover food. That at least is the suggestion, though there may be an element of Downton Abbeyish wishful thinking here. Scrooge's attitude (pre-reformation) to Bob Cratchit's paid holiday on Christmas Day—"A poor excuse for picking a man's pocket every twenty-fifth of December"—may have been more representative.

clutch *v.* 抓住；紧握

7 What is **undeniably** true is that the practice developed of people giving Christmas boxes—commonly a small gift or some money—to tradespeople who had provided them with good service in the course of the year. The Victorians may have given the name to Boxing Day, but this tradition **predates** the 19th century. It was certainly **prevalent** in 17th-century England, as the entry in Samuel Pepys' diary for 19 December 1663 **attests**. "By coach to my shoemaker's and paid all there," he reports, "and gave something to the boys' box against Christmas."

undeniably *adv.* 不可否认地

predate *v.* 在日期上早于（先于）

prevalent *adj.* 流行的，盛行的；广传的；普遍的

attest *v.* 证明；作证

8 The tradition of giving Christmas boxes to tradespeople was still **extant** a generation ago but is now disappearing—a reflection of our increasingly **atomised** and **anonymised** society, and of the move away from a social structure based on **deference** and **patronage**. For better or worse, Christmas really isn't what it used to be.

extant *adj.* 现存的；显著的

atomised *adj.* 分化的

anonymised *adj.* 匿名的

deference *n.* 顺从；尊重

patronage *n.* 赞助；光顾

9 Boxing Day is primarily a British tradition, and the U.K. has exported it to Australia, Canada and New Zealand (in each of which it has become primarily a shopping and sporting day). The term is little used in the U.S., and 26 December is not usually a federal holiday, though it is this year because Christmas Day falls on a Sunday. The 26th is a holiday in western Europe, but most countries designate it the "second day of Christmas" rather than Boxing Day.

10 Just to complicate matters, eastern **orthodox** Christian countries celebrate St. Stephen's Day on 27 December. They do not associate it with Christmas boxes nor, coming from the **chillier** parts of Europe, do they **plunge headlong into** frozen seas and lakes. They go to church, eat and drink **copiously**, and watch the telly instead. How very sensible.

orthodox *adj.* 正统的；东正教的

chilly *adj.* 寒冷的

plunge into 跳入

headlong *adv.* 莽撞地

copiously *adv.* 充裕地，丰富地

Extended Activities

Each of the following statements contains information given in one of the paragraphs in the passage. Identify the paragraph from which the information is derived and put the corresponding number in the space provided.

_____ 1) Boxing day is actually not a holiday in a lot of countries.

_____ 2) On the Feast of Stephen, the Christians should offer care and help to people who are poor and less healthy than them.

_____ 3) St. Stephen's Day became a bank holiday in 1871.

_____ 4) Boxing Day is celebrated two days after Christmas in eastern Christian countries.

_____ 5) There is no consensus about the dating of Boxing Day.

_____ 6) One theory of the origin of Boxing Day is that it was derived from the feast day of St. Stephen.

Decide whether the following statements are true or false. Write T for true and F for false.

_____ 1) Boxing Day has nothing to do with sports, but is closely related to charitable behaviors.

_____ 2) There was story evidence that during the late Roman Empire, money was collected for the poor in alm boxes in honor of St. Stephen.

_____ 3) The practice of giving Christmas boxes was first started in the Victorian period.

_____ 4) The tradition of giving Christmas boxes is now disappearing, which leads to the change in social structure.

_____ 5) Different from some Christian countries, orthodox Christian countries celebrate the day on 27 Dec. by going to church, eating and drinking and watching TV.

Translate the following paragraph into English.

庆祝圣诞节的方式很多。有的英国人去度假，有的下馆子，有的和朋友一起庆祝，但大部分人都认为与家人、亲戚一起待几天才是圣诞节传统的庆祝方式。圣诞节这天人们会享用大量美味的点心，拆看亲人赠送的礼物，这些礼物已在圣诞树下静候多时了，大部分成年人还会开怀畅饮。有些人将去教堂做礼拜或者在电视上观看女王的演讲作为家庭传统的一部分，而大部分人都会在下午或者傍晚下棋打牌或者看电影。经历了激动人心的重大节日之后，大部分人都会在家里开开心心地度过节日，他们会安安静静地享受自己的礼物，然后享用圣诞大餐剩余的美食，比如咖喱火鸡。

Exploring

Work in groups and organize a celebration on campus in honor of a western festival, like Halloween, Thanksgiving or Christmas. Your design of the specific activities can be traditional or original, but remember to make sure the activities really reflect the significance of the festival. Your group work can be divided into the following steps.

Step 1   Search more information about the ways in which western festivals are celebrated.

Step 2   Work out a celebration plan including the time and location, food, activities, costumes and any other preparations.

Step 3   Have your celebration on campus and write a report to share your feelings and experiences with others.

 # Mini-pedia

Saturnalia

Saturnalia, the most popular of Roman festivals, is dedicated to the Roman god Saturn. Now the festival's influence continues to be felt throughout the Western world.

Originally celebrated on December 17, Saturnalia was extended first to three and eventually to seven days. The date has been connected with the winter sowing season, which in modern Italy varies from October to January. Remarkably like the Greek Kronia, it was the liveliest festival of the year. All work and business were suspended. Slaves were given temporary freedom to say and do what they liked, and certain moral restrictions were eased. The streets were infected with a Mardi Gras madness; a mock king was chosen; the seasonal greeting to Saturnalia was heard everywhere. The closing days of the Saturnalia were known as Sigillaria, because of the custom of making, toward the end of the festival, presents of candles, wax models of fruit, and waxen statuettes which were fashioned by the Sigillaria or manufacturers of small figures in wax and other media. The cult statue of Saturn himself, traditionally bound at the feet with woolen bands, was untied, presumably to come out and join the fun.

The influence of the Saturnalia upon the celebrations of Christmas and the New Year has been direct. The fact that Christmas was celebrated on the birthday of the unconquered sun gave the season a solar background, connected with the Kalends of January (January 1, the Roman New Year) when houses were decorated with greenery and lights, and presents were given to children and the poor. Concerning the gift candles, the Romans had a story that an old prophecy bade the earliest inhabitants of Latium send the heads to Hades and phota to Saturn. The ancient Latins interpreted this to mean human sacrifices, but, according to legend, Hercules advised using lights (phos means "light" or "man" according to the accent) and not human heads.

 # Reflection

Achievements	Yes	No
I can describe how people celebrate festivals, especially some western festivals.		
I have understood how the ways in which people celebrate festivals have changed.		
I am aware of the significance of western festivals.		
I have acquired useful words and expressions related to festivals.		

UNIT 7
ETIQUETTE

◆

GOALS

1 To understand the importance of etiquette;

2 To know what good manners and good breeding are;

3 To become aware of the differences between good manners and good breeding;

4 To learn some important tips on international business;

5 To acquire some words and expressions about etiquette.

Warming-up

Answer the following questions:

1. How do you understand good manners and good breeding? What do they mean respectively?
2. Why is etiquette important in all walks of life?
3. What do you know about Jonathan Swift?

Reading

Passage One A Treatise on Good Manners and Good Breeding

By Jonathan Swift

❶   Good manners is the art of making those people easy with whom we converse.

❷   Whoever makes the fewest persons uneasy is the best bred in the company.

❸   As the best law is founded upon reason, so are the best manners. And as some lawyers have introduced unreasonable things into common law, so likewise many teachers have introduced absurd things into common good manners.

❹   One principal point of this art is to suit our behavior to three several degrees of men: our superiors, our equals, and those below us.

❺   For instance, to press either of the two former to eat or drink is a **breach** of manners; but a farmer or a tradesman must be thus treated, or else it will be difficult to persuade them that they are welcome.

6 Pride, ill nature, and want of sense, are the three great sources of ill manners; without some one of these defects, no man will behave himself ill for want of experience; or of what, in the language of fools, is called knowing the world.

7 I defy any one to assign an incident wherein reason will not direct us what we are to say or do in company, if we are not misled by pride or ill nature.

8 Therefore I insist that good sense is the principal foundation of good manners; but because the former is a gift which very few among mankind are possessed of, therefore all the civilized nations of the world have agreed upon fixing some rules for common behavior, best suited to their general customs, or fancies, as a kind of artificial good sense, to supply the defects of reason.

9 As the common forms of good manners were intended for regulating the conduct of those who have weak understandings; so they have been corrupted by the persons for whose use they were contrived. For these people have fallen into a needless and endless way of **multiplying** ceremonies, which have been extremely troublesome to those who practice them, and insupportable to everybody else: insomuch that wise men are often more uneasy at the over **civility** of these refiners, than they could possibly be in the conversations of peasants or mechanics.

10 The **impertinencies** of this ceremonial behavior are nowhere better seen than at those tables where ladies **preside**, who value themselves upon account of their good breeding; where a man must reckon upon passing an hour without doing any one thing he has a mind to, unless he will be so hardy to break through all the settled **decorum** of the family. She determines what he loves best, and how much he shall eat; and if the master of the house happens to be of the same **disposition**, he proceeds in the same **tyrannical**

breach *n.* 违反，违背

multiply *v.* 增加

civility *n.* 客气；礼貌

impertinency *n.* 不合理

preside *v.* 主持

decorum *n.* 礼节，礼仪

disposition *n.* 性情；性格

tyrannical *adj.* 专制的；专横的

manner to prescribe in the drinking part: at the same time, you are under the necessity of answering a thousand apologies for your entertainment. And although a good deal of this humor is pretty well worn off among many people of the best fashion, yet too much of it still remains, especially in the country; where an honest gentleman assured me, that having been kept four days, against his will, at a friend's house, with all the circumstances of hiding his boots, locking up the stable, and other contrivances of the like nature, he could not remember, from the moment he came into the house to the moment he left it, any one thing, wherein his inclination was not directly contradicted; as if the whole family had entered into a combination to **torment** him.

torment *v.* 折磨

⑪   But, besides all this, it would be endless to recount the many foolish and ridiculous accidents I have observed among these unfortunate **proselytes** to ceremony. I have seen a duchess fairly knocked down, by the **precipitancy** of an **officious** coxcomb running to save her the trouble of opening a door. I remember, upon a birthday at court, a great lady was utterly desperate by a dish of sauce let fall by a page directly upon her head-dress and brocade, while she gave a sudden turn to her elbow upon some point of ceremony with the person who sat next her. Monsieur Buys, the Dutch envoy, whose politics and manners were much of a size, brought a son with him, about thirteen years old, to a great table at court. The boy and his father, whatever they put on their plates, they first offered round in order, to every person in the company; so that we could not get a minute's quiet during the whole dinner. At last their two plates happened to encounter, and with so much violence, that, being china, they broke in twenty pieces, and stained half the company with wet **sweetmeats** and cream.

proselyte *n.* 信奉者
precipitancy *n.* 急躁，贸然
officious *adj.* 过分殷勤的

sweetmeat *n.* 甜食

⑫   There is a **pedantry** in manners, as in all arts and sciences; and sometimes in trades. Pedantry is properly the overrating any kind of knowledge we pretend to. And if that kind of knowledge be a trifle in itself, the pedantry is the greater. For which reason I look upon fiddlers, dancing-masters, heralds, masters of the ceremony, etc. to be greater pedants than Lipsius, or the elder

pedantry *n.* 迂腐；卖弄学问

Scaliger. With these kind of pedants, the court, while I knew it, was always plentifully stocked. I mean from the gentleman usher (at least) inclusive, downward to the gentleman porter; who are, generally speaking, the most insignificant race of people that this island can afford, and with the smallest **tincture** of good manners, which is the only trade they profess. For being wholly illiterate, and conversing chiefly with each other, they reduce the whole system of breeding within the forms and circles of their several offices; and as they are below the notice of ministers, they live and die in court under all revolutions with great **obsequiousness** to those who are in any degree of favour or credit, and with rudeness or insolence to everybody else. Whence I have long concluded, that good manners are not a plant of the court growth; for if they were, those people who have understandings directly of a level for such acquirements, and who have served such long apprenticeships to nothing else, would certainly have picked them up. For as to the great officers, who attend the prince's person or councils, or preside in his family, they are a **transient** body, who have no better a title to good manners than their neighbours, nor will probably have recourse to gentlemen ushers for instruction. So that I know little to be learnt at court upon this head, except in the material circumstance of dress; wherein the authority of the maids of honour must indeed be allowed to be almost equal to that of a favourite actress.

tincture *n.* 一丝，些微

obsequiousness *n.* 阿谀，奉承

transient *adj.* 暂时的，临时的

⑬　I remember a passage my Lord Bolingbroke told me, that going to receive Prince Eugene of Savoy at his landing, in order to conduct him immediately to the Queen, the prince said, he was much concerned that he could not see her Majesty that night; for Monsieur Hoffman (who was then by) had assured his Highness that he could not be admitted into her presence with a tied-up periwig; that his equipage was not arrived; and that he had endeavoured in vain to borrow a long one among all his valets and pages. My lord turned the matter into a jest, and brought the Prince to her Majesty; for which he was highly censured by the whole tribe of gentlemen ushers; among whom Monsieur Hoffman, an old dull resident of the Emperor's, had picked up this material point of ceremony; and which, I believe, was the best lesson he had learned in five-and-twenty years' residence.

14 I make a difference between good manners and good breeding; although, in order to vary my expression, I am sometimes forced to **confound** them. By the first, I only understand the art of remembering and applying certain settled forms of general behaviour. But good breeding is of a much larger extent; for besides an uncommon degree of literature sufficient to qualify a gentleman for reading a play, or a political pamphlet, it takes in a great compass of knowledge; no less than that of dancing, fighting, gaming, making the circle of Italy, riding the great horse, and speaking French; not to mention some other secondary, or **subaltern** accomplishments, which are more easily acquired. So that the difference between good breeding and good manners lies in this, that the former cannot be attained to by the best understandings, without study and labour; whereas a tolerable degree of reason will instruct us in every part of good manners, without other assistance.

confound *v.* 混淆

subaltern *adj.* 次要的，低等的

15 First, a necessary part of good manners, is a punctual observance of time at our own dwellings, or those of others, or at third places; whether upon matter of civility, business, or diversion; which rule, though it be a plain dictate of common reason, yet the greatest minister I ever knew was the greatest **trespasser** against it; by which all his business doubled upon him, and placed him in a continual arrear. Upon which I often used to rally him, as deficient in point of good manners. I have known more than one ambassador, and secretary of state with a very moderate portion of intellectuals, execute their offices with good success and applause, by the mere force of exactness and regularity. If you duly observe time for the service of another, it doubles the obligation; if upon your own account, it would be manifest folly, as well as ingratitude, to neglect it. If both are concerned, to make your equal or inferior attend on you, to his own disadvantage, is pride and injustice.

trespasser *n.* 违反者

⑯ Ignorance of forms cannot properly be styled ill manners; because forms are subject to frequent changes; and consequently, being not founded upon reason, are beneath a wise man's regard. Besides, they vary in every country; and after a short period of time, very frequently in the same; so that a man who travels, must needs be at first a stranger to them in every court through which he passes; and perhaps at his return, as much a stranger in his own; and after all, they are easier to be remembered or forgotten than faces or names.

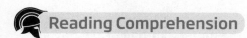

Reading Comprehension

Decide whether the following statements are true or false. Write T for true and F for false.

_____ 1) In terms of appropriate behavior, to force a farmer or a tradesman to eat or drink is good mannered or else they will think they are unwelcome.

_____ 2) Good manners are merely the art of remembering and applying certain settled forms of general behavior while good breeding cannot be attained to by the best understanding without hard study or accumulating various knowledge.

_____ 3) The unnecessary and endless multiplied ceremonies make those who practice them feel uneasy.

_____ 4) If you want to be a good mannered person, you should first observe punctuality.

_____ 5) The author once saw a duchess knocked down by a rash man who ran to open the door only to flatter her.

_____ 6) Not knowing the settled forms of general behavior is sure to be regarded as ill mannered.

_____ 7) Prince Eugene of Savoy was worried that he could not see the Queen because he wore a wig.

_____ 8) People often show their bad manners because of pride, bad temper and lacking sense instead of lack of experience or of knowing the world.

_____ 9) The author was once assured by an honest gentleman that his friend's whole family united to torture him.

_____ 10) There is a pedantry in all arts and sciences, in trades sometimes as well as in manners.

2 Below is a short passage with several incomplete sentences. Please fill in the blanks with appropriate words based on the context meaning.

The four terms of courtesy which are most frequently used in western societies are "_____," "_____", "_____", and "_____". In an imperative sentence, once "_____" is used, the tone would be more polite and pleasant. Whenever others do something for you, you should always show your gratitude by saying "_____". "_____" and "_____" are frequently used terms to express one's apology. For instance, if you have to refuse someone's good intention, or say something that sounds disagreeable to them, a "_____" will make them feel less uncomfortable. And if you disturb others with unnecessary noise in public, such as coughing, _____, yawning or _____, you should say "_____".

3 Answer the following questions based on the understanding of the passage.

1) How does the author Jonathan Swift differentiate good manners and good breeding? Do you agree with him?
2) What examples does Jonathan Swift illustrate in the passage to satirize the unnecessary formalities?
3) What are the author's suggestions on good manners?
4) Can you identify Swift's humor in the passage?

Language in Use

4 Fill in the blanks with the words from the word bank. Make changes when necessary.

confound	pedantry	torment	officious	preside
multiply	breach	decorum	contrive	disposition

1) There is no virtue in autonomy which may prove empty and high virtue in cooperative arrangements which _____ resources without sacrifice of essential freedom.
2) China is a land of _____ with a 5,000-year history. Beijing is a capital of civility, a city of millions of citizens putting propriety into daily practice.
3) He had a reputation for being politically _____ and self-serving.
4) To _____ two things means not to be able to tell them apart.
5) The twin brothers are alike in appearance but differ greatly in _____.
6) How can a merciful God permit a human being to suffer such _____?

7) A skillful cook, who understands how to oblige his guests, will _____ to make it as expensive as they please.

8) He had all the illumination of wisdom and none of its _____.

9) Police arrested the demonstrators for committing a _____ of the peace.

10) It's a great pleasure for me to _____ at this dinner in honor of Chairman Smith.

 Translate the following paragraph into Chinese.

First, a necessary part of good manners, is a punctual observance of time at our own dwellings, or those of others, or at third places; whether upon matter of civility, business, or diversion; which rule, though it be a plain dictate of common reason, yet the greatest minister I ever knew was the greatest trespasser against it; by which all his business doubled upon him, and placed him in a continual arrear. Upon which I often used to rally him, as deficient in point of good manners. I have known more than one ambassador, and secretary of state with a very moderate portion of intellectuals, execute their offices with good success and applause, by the mere force of exactness and regularity. If you duly observe time for the service of another, it doubles the obligation; if upon your own account, it would be manifest folly, as well as ingratitude, to neglect it. If both are concerned, to make your equal or inferior attend on you, to his own disadvantage, is pride and injustice.

 Oral Practice

 It is believed that good manners are symbolic of good education, but others argue that good manners in excess will make people feel uncomfortable. What's your opinion of the delicate employment of good manners in intercultural context? You may use the words and expressions in the following box.

common civilization core	universal values	cultural differences
communication patterns	high/low context communication	
social norms	social rules	self-independence
personal privacy	empathy	comply with...
pragmatic errors	aggressive	show respect for...
dominant	intrude upon	adapt... to...

Passage Two Broadening Global Awareness

By Pamela Eyring

1 Success in the international arena starts with understanding of customs and etiquettes. As the international marketplace flourishes, employees are being asked to do more, and with the diversity in the workforce higher than ever and offshoring becoming a **viable** option, understanding different cultures will prove invaluable.

viable *adj.* 切实可行的

2 Listed below are 10 tips to achieve success in the international business arena. They reinforce the talents you already possess and provide valuable soft skills to help you compete in a global economy that demands mental flexibility and awareness. You can use **protocol** and personal diplomacy to tip the scales in your favor no matter where you conduct business.

protocol *n.* 礼仪

Tip 1: Perfect your greetings and introductions.

3 When meeting someone for the first time, you will make a lasting impression on that person within the first few seconds of your greeting. Style and form play a major role in successfully conducting business meetings worldwide. Regardless of the setting, introductions and greetings are an essential element of proper business etiquette.

4 When you introduce yourself, include your first and last name, your title, and company name. "Good morning, my name is Mary Davis. I'm the vice president of Doe Imports."

5 Wait to be introduced. Be polite and modest, and wait until the verbal introduction concludes before extending your hand for a handshake. But remain alert and immediately extend your hand if the other person offers hers before the introduction is complete.

6 Avoid saying "hi" and "hello". These greetings are too casual in international business settings. Saying "hello" with their name is more professional.

Tip 2: Be a world-class handshaker.

7 Customs differ in select countries, but the American handshake, toned down a bit, is accepted worldwide.

8 Most Europeans shake hands on arrival and departure. Their grip is light, not firm. In parts of Europe, handshakes last twice as long as U.S. handshakes: five to seven strokes. Pulling your hand away too soon creates an impression of rejection.

9 Always shake hands with the oldest person or the one of senior rank first, and then proceed on down the line of authority. The higher-ranking person extends his hand first; the lesser-ranking person receives the extended hand. Count on your host to make the necessary introductions in the protocol of handshaking. Make sure every meeting, business or social, begins and ends with a handshake.

Tip 3: Know eye contact etiquette.

10 In the United States, Americans believe that good eye contact is important during business and social conversations. Direct eye contact is a sign of openness, honesty, and assertiveness. Consider cultural differences before departing for another country.

11 In parts of the Middle East and North Africa, eye contact is intense. People of Arabic descent look deeply into a person's eyes to search the soul and take measure of a personality.

12 In Thailand, eye contact is used to **facilitate** daily activities. If you're in a restaurant and need the server, all you'll have to do is catch his eye and raise your eyebrows to get instant service.

facilitate *v.* 推动，促进

13 In Mexico and Puerto Rico, however, direct eye contact is considered an aggressive gesture. And in Japan, direct eye contact is considered slightly **intimidating**. However, well-traveled Japanese have studied western culture and make direct eye contact and offer a firm handshake.

intimidate *v.* 恐吓，威胁

Tip 4: Dress appropriately.

⑭　Business attire in the international arena consists of quality fabrics and conservative styling in **subdued** colors. Dress in an understated style, regardless of your gender. The best known business look in the United States is the Wall Street look. It does not make a fashion statement, but it does have a style that works worldwide. The Wall Street look is not meant to express individuality, but rather to show status in its quality.

subdued *adj.* 柔和的

Tip 5: Know body language and gestures.

⑮　The ability to communicate is the key to your success. Be aware of the body language of your international colleagues, and reinforce your position by knowing and using the body language of your client.

⑯　Asians avoid any physical contact except a handshake. Keep a distance of at least three feet during conversation. Do not move closer if they back away from you. Britons and Western Europeans avoid excessive hand gestures, touching, and standing too close. Europeans, Latin Americans, and Arabs will stand close together during conversation. Resist the urge to back away to your comfort zone. Americans consider an arm's length as sufficient distance while conversing. Don't interpret this as formal. Body language in the United States is very casual by world standards.

Tip 6: Use proper titles.

⑰　When someone has a title, such as senator, governor, or commander, use it correctly. Research the titles of those with whom you will interact.

Tip 7: Understand rank and status.

⑱　When visiting another country, be prepared for a formal atmosphere in your business dealings. Codes of etiquette may be elaborate and inflexible in ways you will not encounter in the United States. An awareness of proper behavior is expected inside and outside the office as well as sensitivity to cultural differences that signal rank and status and how they affect your business relationship.

19 Your rank in the organization will determine whom you meet in the host country. A manager from the United States will meet with a manager in the host country. Your corporate title may have a different connotation in your host country. Research titles to make sure your position is not lower than the position of the person you are meeting.

20 Sending a mid-level executive to deal with a high-ranking executive in your host country is interpreted as an insult. The message is clear—you and your company consider the executive or the business itself to be of little importance.

Tip 8: Use business card etiquette.

21 Your business card represents you and your company. Its printing and paper quality should be consistent with the image you wish to convey.

22 Men and women should carry cards in a card case. Place several cards in your outside jacket pocket for easy access before attending an event. Present your card with your right hand or both hands, with the card's host-language side up and the print facing the recipient so the recipient can read it.

23 Take your time and look at the card. It is representative of the person. In Asian countries, take the card with both hands and read it thoroughly. Place the guest's card in an appropriate and respectful place.

24 Place your card in your card case, or in your outside or inside jacket pockets. Never place it in your back trouser pocket because this is considered offensive in some cultures. Don't write on the card in the person's presence. This is considered rude in some cultures.

Tip 9: Know global conversation skills.

25　Pay attention to the volume of voices around you. If necessary, readjust your voice to a lower level to match the others. Raising your voice won't help the person understand you better.

26　Don't interrupt when someone is speaking. Don't finish someone's sentence. Both acts project rudeness and impatience, which results in losing information and business.

27　Don't ask, "Do you understand me?" It's annoying and demeaning. Many people choose to agree rather than appear as if they don't understand you.

28　Keep still. Too many body movements are annoying and distracting. Refrain from shuffling papers or **fidgeting** with your pen or other objects.

fidget v. 烦躁，不安

29　Prepare yourself in advance to discuss your host country or the homeland of your visitor. Read publications devoted to international news.

Tip 10: Review gift-giving dos and don'ts.

30　Gift-giving customs vary from one country to another. An appropriate gift in a European country may be inappropriate in an Asian country.

31　Many companies in the United States have a policy that doesn't allow employees to give or receive gifts, or establishes a maximum value on gifts given and received. A visitor should not be offended if someone can't accept a gift. Always check with the embassy of your host country for guidelines. Some examples of appropriate gifts to give someone from Latin America include fine chocolates, a logo gift, or a handsome art book.

Extended Activities

Each of the following statements contains information given in one of the paragraphs in the passage. Identify the paragraph from which the information is derived and put the corresponding number in the space provided.

_____ 1) Prevent yourself from fidgeting or showing nervousness or embarrassment by making too many body movements.

_____ 2) Try to say "hello" with their name when greeting in international business settings, which is more professional.

_____ 3) Your rank in the organization should be counterpart with that of the person you will meet in the host country.

_____ 4) When presenting your card to the guest you should use your right hand or both hands.

_____ 5) The person with the higher rank often offers his hand first, and the lower ranking person receives the extended hand.

_____ 6) A visitor should not feel annoyed if someone can't accept a gift.

_____ 7) If you want to get instant service in a restaurant in Thailand, what you have to do is to catch the waitress' eye and raise your eyebrows.

_____ 8) Try to keep a distance of at least three feet when conversing with Asians for they don't like physical contact except a handshake.

_____ 9) It would be considered very offensive to put the card in your back trouser pocket in some cultures.

_____ 10) Style and form play a significant role in successfully conducting business meetings worldwide.

Decide whether the statements are true or false according to the passage. Write T for true and F for false.

_____ 1) An appropriate gift in a European country is always appropriate in other Asian countries.

_____ 2) It will be interpreted as an insult if you send a mid-level executive to deal with a high-ranking executive in your host country.

_____ 3) Handshaking customs vary from country to country.

_____ 4) Britons and Europeans like standing close together during their conversation and they like using a lot of hand gestures as well.

_____ 5) Raise your voice a little higher so as to make yourself better understood.

_____ 6) Present your card with your right hand or both hands, with the card's host-language side down and the print facing yourself.

_____ 7) In terms of business attire the dress style of Wall Street is considered acceptable worldwide.

_____ 8) You should immediately extend your hand for shaking if the other person offers his/hers, even if the verbal introduction isn't complete.

Translate the following paragraph into English.

礼仪之于社会正如衣服（apparel）对人一样重要。没有衣服的遮掩，人们会以裸体（nudity）示人，从而导致道德的败坏。没有礼节（proprieties）约束，社会会陷入悲惨的境地，人们必要的交流（intercourse）会被多余的提防和麻烦所破坏。如果社会是一辆火车，那么礼节就是它的铁轨，让火车滚滚前进；如果社会是一辆马车，那么礼节就是它的轮子和轴，支撑它前行。礼节的缺失让一对最亲密的朋友变成不死不休的敌人，甚至让友邦兵刃相向。我们从人类的历史上可以找出很多的例子。因此我建议你在任何人面前都要站在礼节的角度，尽力不要做有违礼节的事情，以免冒犯别人或树敌。

Exploring

Work in pairs and make up dialogues according to the following situation: Li Hua is a new staff in an international organization. This is his first day working in the office. After the first day of work, he was invited to attend a welcome party organized by the company. Design a dialogue between Li Hua and his colleagues. Your dialogue should include the following points. You may refer to what you've learned in Passage Two for your reference.

- Li Hua's self-introduction to the colleagues;
- Li Hua's inquiry about the customs and etiquettes in the international arena;
- The colleagues' suggestions on how to achieve success in the international business arena.

Mini-pedia

Do You Know?

Top Ten Table Manner Tips
1. Place your napkin in your lap.
2. Turn off your phone.
3. Wait for everyone to be served before eating.
4. Use a knife and fork to cut meat.
5. Cut your food one piece at a time.
6. Chew with your mouth closed.
7. Don't reach across the table.
8. Don't talk with your mouth full.
9. Don't pick your teeth at the table.
10. Say "excuse me" when leaving the table.

Ten Essential Tips for Business Dining Etiquette
1. Choose the right restaurant.
2. Arrive on time.
3. Turn off your smartphone.
4. Introduce yourself.
5. Come prepared with well-informed small talk.
6. Never assume your client is looking for a social encounter.
7. Avoid expensive or market price items.
8. Always be kind to the wait staff.
9. Don't drink or limit yourself to one drink.
10. Whoever initiates the dinner should pay for it.

Reflection

Achievements	Yes	No
I got to know the importance of etiquette.		
I have understood the differences between good manners and good breeding.		
I have learned some important tips on international business.		
I have acquired useful words and expressions related to etiquette.		

UNIT 8
WEDDING

◇

GOALS

1 To know the practice and customs of a western wedding ceremony;

2 To understand cultural meanings behind the practice and customs of a western wedding ceremony;

3 To become aware of the differences in practice and customs between China and the U.K.;

4 To acquire related words and expressions about wedding ceremonies.

Warming-up

Answer the following questions:

1. What does the old saying "Something Old, Something New, Something Borrowed, Something Blue" mean?

2. What do you know about Prince William and Catherine's wedding?

3. What does a wedding ring symbolize?

Reading

Passage One William and Catherine's Wedding

❶   With her father, Michael Middleton proudly at her left side, and her sister Philippa supporting the train as Maid of Honour, Catherine stepped into Westminster Abbey looking gracefully beautiful and **radiant**. A brief stop in front of the grave of the Unknown Warrior, gave Philippa the chance to arrange the 2.7 metre train of Catherine's stunning wedding dress behind her. Meanwhile, William and Harry exited Westminster Abbey's traditional groom's waiting area at Saint Edmund's Chapel and walked to the Abbey's **altar**, where William looked straight ahead. His brother Harry, standing on his right hand side, provided a few words of **commentary** or **reassurance** as William waited patiently for his bride to complete her walk up the aisle.

radiant *adj.* 容光焕发的

altar *n.* 圣坛

commentary *n.* 评论

reassurance *n.* 安心

❷ Catherine began her procession along the 100 yards of red carpet on her Father's arm, past the impressive trees which had especially been brought in to Westminster Abbey, to the sound of Sir Charles Parry's **coronation anthem**, "I was glad when they said unto me: We will go into the House of the Lord", based on *Psalm 122 verses 1 to 3* and *6 to 7*. Philippa followed behind Catherine with the bridesmaids and pages.

coronation *n.* 加冕；加冕礼
anthem *n.* 圣歌

❸ As Catherine joined him on his left hand side at the altar at the top of the aisle, William was able to take his first look at his bride in her wedding dress. Lip readers say that he told her "you look beautiful", and that a few moments later there at the altar he joked to Catherine's father Michael Middleton, saying "We were supposed to have just a small family affair!"

❹ After the Hymn of "Guide me O Though Great Redeemer", the Dean gave his Welcome and Introduction, including the words "if any man can **shew** any just cause why they may not lawfully be joined together, let him now speak, or else hereafter for ever hold his peace". There was a brief silence, as the **Archbishop** of Canterbury took his place in front of the couple for the **solemnization** of the marriage. Both William and Catherine said "I will". The Archbishop asked "Who giveth this woman to be married to this man?" Standing on Catherine's left, her father, Michael Middleton took Catherine's right hand and passed it to the Archbishop, who in turn passed her hand to Prince William. Hand in hand, the couple said their vows to each other before Harry gave the Archbishop the ring, which the Archbishop then blessed. Following a long tradition, the ring has been fashioned from Welsh gold given to Prince William by the Queen. William placed the ring on Catherine's finger. For a moment it looked like it might not go on all the way past her **knuckle** but a gentle push and on it went. William said "With this ring I thee wed; with my body I thee honour; and all my worldly goods with thee I share: in the name of the Father, and of the Son, and of the Holy Ghost. Amen", at which point the couple kneeled and the Archbishop said a prayer with the **congregation**, asking for God's blessing that the couple may keep

shew *v.* 表示

archbishop *n.* 大主教

solemnization *n.* 庄重

knuckle *n.* 指关节

congregation *n.* 集会，集合；
人群

their vows and live in perfect love and peace together.

5   Removing a piece of cloth known as a **stole** from his neck, the Archbishop wrapped William and Catherine's right hands gently together and raised them, binding them together in the sight of God, and said "Those whom God hath joined together let no man put **asunder**." Then, after the Archbishop had removed the stole, he pronounced William and Catherine to be man and wife. Sounds of crowds cheering from outside could be heard. The Archbishop said a prayer in which he asked that God may bless them and look with favour upon them that they may live together with God's grace and **benediction**.

> stole *n.* 圣衣
>
> asunder *adj.* 分离的
>
> benediction *n.* 祝福，赐福

6   The hymn, "Love Divine All Loves Excelling" by Charles Wesley followed, as William and Catherine walked off toward two chairs on the right hand side of the Abbey, and picked up their programs to sing.

7   From one of the **pulpits**, Catherine's brother James Middleton gave an impressively delivered reading from *Romans 12:1,2,9–18* as the lesson, as the **newlyweds** exchanged reassuring glances between each other. This was followed by *the Anthem* by John Rutter, specially **commissioned** by the Dean and Chapter of Westminster for the Royal wedding.

> pulpit *n.* 讲道坛
>
> newlyweds *n.* 新婚夫妇
>
> commission *v.* 委任

8   Then the couple and their witnesses Philippa Middleton, Camilla, Prince Charles, Michael, Carole and James Middleton temporarily disappeared from all view, even that of the television cameras, moving into the Shrine of St Edward the Confessor, which has been there since the Middle Ages and is the most **sacred** part of Westminster Abbey. There they signed the three marriage registers in private: 2 as part of the Abbey collection plus the Chapel Royal register which is kept by officials at the Chapel Royal. The Marriage Certificate was also completed there. Whilst the newlyweds and witnesses were out of view, the choir sang *Best Pair of Sirens* by Charles Parry, adapted from John Milton's poem "At a Solemn Musick".

> sacred *adj.* 神圣的

9 The registers signed, all the witnesses apart from Best Man, Harry, and Maid of Honour, Philippa emerged from the Shrine as the choir continued their hymn. The Archbishop began the procession back down the red-carpeted aisle and the **trumpeters** of the Central Band of the Royal Air Force sounded the fanfare: *The Valiant and Brave*, followed by sound of The London Chamber **Orchestra** playing *Crown Imperial* by William Walton as the newlyweds emerged from the Shrine of St Edward the Confessor, followed by Harry and Philippa. After a bow from William to his grandmother, the Queen, and a **curtsey** from Catherine to her new grandmother-in-law, the royal couple made their procession hand in hand back down the length of the tree-lined aisle, followed by two bridesmaids, two pages, and then Harry and Philippa, Prince Charles and Carole, and Camilla and Michael. Smiles shone brightly from both William and Catherine as they made their way down the red carpet—their clear love and **adoration** for one another now united in the **sanctity** of marriage in this wonderful service.

trumpeter *n.* 小号手

valiant *adj.* 勇敢的
orchestra *n.* 管弦乐队

curtsey *n.* 屈膝礼

adoration *n.* 爱慕
sanctity *n.* 神圣不可侵犯

10 After the service, the newlyweds travelled in an open-topped carriage for the 15-minute journey from Westminster Abbey to Buckingham Palace, past London landmarks, including the Houses of Parliament, Big Ben and Horse Guards Parade. More than 1,000 military personnel and musicians lined the procession route while 500,000 well-wishers gathered outside the palace. Thousands of street parties were held around the U.K., and big screens were put up in many towns and cities. The BBC has been bringing viewers and listeners comprehensive coverage across TV, radio and online, in the U.K. and around the world.

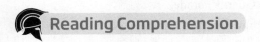

Reading Comprehension

⭐ **Decide whether the following statements are true or false. Write T for true and F for false.**

_____ **1)** William and Catherine's wedding was held in St. Paul's Cathedral.

_____ **2)** The wedding ring has been fashioned from Welsh gold given to Prince

William by the Queen.

_____ 3) Catherine's brother James Middleton gave an impressively delivered reading from *Romans 12:1,2,9–19* as the lesson after the Archbishop pronounced William and Catherine to be man and wife.

_____ 4) William and Catherine signed the three marriage registers in private: 2 as part of the Abbey collection plus the Chapel Royal register which is kept by officials at the Chapel Royal.

_____ 5) On the wedding day, more than 50,000 well-wishers gathered outside Buckingham Palace to celebrate this big event.

Complete the sentences with the information from the passage.

1) Catherine's sister Philippa, as _____, had a chance to arrange the 2.7 metre train of Catherine's stunning wedding dress when Catherine stopped in front of the grave of the Unknown Warrior.

2) With this ring I thee wed; with my body I thee honour; and all my worldly goods with thee I share: in the name of _____, _____, and of the Holy Ghost. Amen!

3) Then, after the Archbishop had removed the stole, he pronounced William and Catherine to be _____.

4) Then the couple and their witnesses Philippa Middleton, Camilla, Prince Charles, Michael, Carole and James Middleton temporarily moved into the Shrine of St Edward the Confessor to _____. The Marriage Certificate was also completed there.

5) More than 1,000 _____ lined the procession route while 500,000 well-wishers gathered outside the palace.

Put the following sentences in the right order according to the development of the royal wedding.

A. Then, after the Archbishop had removed the stole, he pronounced William and Catherine to be man and wife.

B. The newlyweds travelled in an open-topped carriage for the 15-minute journey from Westminster Abbey to Buckingham Palace, past London landmarks, including the Houses of Parliament, Big Ben and Horse Guards Parade.

C. After a bow from William to his grandmother, the Queen, and a curtsey from Catherine to her new grandmother-in-law, the royal couple made their procession hand in hand back down the length of the tree-lined aisle.

D. Catherine stepped into Westminster Abbey with her father, Michael Middleton proudly at her left side.

E. William and Catherine signed the three marriage registers in private and completed the Marriage Certificate.

F. The Archbishop asked "Who giveth this woman to be married to this man?"

G. Hand in hand, the couple said their vows to each other before Harry gave the Archbishop the ring, which the Archbishop then blessed.

(   ) —— (   ) —— (   ) —— (   ) —— (   ) —— (   ) —— (   )

Language in Use

Fill in the blanks with the words from the word bank. Make changes when necessary.

radiant	reassurance	commentary	register	commission
adoration	comprehensive	procession	sacred	pronounce

1) They provide an interesting _____ on how America's government, people, and artists have chosen to represent their history.

2) If we do not study the problem _____ and come up with a counter-measure, the development of the national economy and the stability of society will be affected.

3) In many instances, this can only be achieved through the subtle differences of intonations and _____.

4) They should be required to _____, pay their taxes, pay a fine and learn English.

5) "I think you need to take care of your skin," he says, "make it more _____. "

6) Following their meal, a carriage _____ will convey the royal party to Buckingham Palace.

7) The Federal Reserve took extraordinary action over the weekend to try to _____ shaky financial markets.

8) So on this solemn day, at this _____ hour, once more we pause.

9) There are so many _____ animals out there, but they all need a home.

10) The _____will vote on the agreement at its next meeting scheduled June 14.

Translate the following paragraphs into Chinese.

With her father, Michael Middleton proudly at her left side, and her sister Philippa supporting the train as Maid of Honour, Catherine stepped into Westminster Abbey looking gracefully beautiful and radiant. A brief stop in front of the grave of the Unknown Warrior, gave Philippa the chance to arrange the 2.7 metre train of Catherine's stunning wedding dress behind her.

Meanwhile, William and Harry exited Westminster Abbey's traditional groom's waiting area at Saint Edmund's Chapel and walked to the Abbey's altar, where William looked straight ahead. His brother Harry, standing on his right hand side, provided a few words of commentary or reassurance as William waited patiently for his bride to complete her walk up the aisle.

 Oral Practice

Read the passage again and discuss with your partner about the most impressive part of William and Catherine's wedding. You may use the following expressions in your discussion.

| Maid of honor | stunning | groomsmen | train of wedding dress |
| wedding ring | vows | archbishop | Marriage Certificate |

Passage Two   Wedding Symbols

❶   Although most weddings are performed for their religious significance, you may be surprised to know that several wedding symbols originated from pagan or decidedly non-religious roots. Many wedding symbols can trace their origins to ancient times while others are more recent additions to wedding traditions.

Wedding Rings

❷   The practice of wearing wedding rings is thought to have started with the Egyptians in 3000 BC. The first rings were made of braided **hemp** and Romans later constructed their wedding rings of iron. Certainly, the circle of a ring represents undying love and the continually renewed vows of the married couple. Circles have long been **archetypes** for not only timelessness, but also wholeness and homecoming. The circle also speaks to the constant round of

hemp *n.* 烟卷

archetype *n.* 原型

the heavens, as well as the eternal return of the seasons, marked by **cyclical** ritual and celebration.

cyclical *adj.* 周期的，循环的

❸　In addition, the circle in rock art, sacred stone arrays, and **astrology** represents both the Sun and the Moon, themselves astrological and **alchemical** symbols for the **masculine** and **feminine** aspects of the **cosmos**. This correspondence with the Sun and Moon is emphasized by the frequent practice of choosing gold for one **betrothed** and silver for the other, as gold and silver are the metals long associated with the Sun and Moon respectively.

astrology *n.* 占星
alchemical *adj.* 炼金术的
masculine *adj.* 男性的；阳性的
feminine *adj.* 女性的；阴性的
cosmos *n.* 宇宙
betroth *v.* 订婚

❹　Rings in general have a deeply rooted magical significance. Enchanted rings figure in many ancient folk tales. **Incantations** and spells for the protection of the wearer of rings are common **motifs**. Today, in traditional religious ceremonies, Christian and otherwise, the wedding rings are blessed by a minister or priest, thus continuing the symbolic practice of **imbuing** rings with protective powers.

incantation *n.* 咒语，符咒

motif *n.* 图案

imbue *v.* 灌输；渗透

❺　Wedding rings have most commonly been worn on the fourth finger of the left hand. **Speculation** has it that this is because the Romans believed that a **vein** ran directly from this finger to the heart. An alternate suggestion for this tradition is that each finger on the hand is associated with a planet in the ancient systems of astrology, and the ring finger of the left hand was associated with the Sun. In this way, the wearing of a wedding ring on that finger signifies the public **proclamation** of the union in the daylight, in other words, the conscious and clearly visible world of human community.

speculation *n.* 推测
vein *n.* 血管

proclamation *n.* 公告，宣布

❻　Wedding rings capture the full range of the ceremonial, symbolic, and communal aspects of marriage, and preserve these many levels of significance as a durable and constant reminder. Ancient yet contemporary, steeped in **lore** and mystery yet almost universally exchanged, wedding rings combine the art of the jeweler, the **reverence** of the betrothed, and the beauty.

lore *n.* 传说

reverence *n.* 尊敬

Wedding Cakes

7   Wedding cakes originated in ancient Rome and were once made from wheat or barley. More like a type of bread, the bride was hit over the head with the cake to make her **fertile**. Wedding guests were encouraged to gather the pieces of cake as they fell and keep them for good luck.

fertile *adj.* 生育的

Symbolism of Groomsmen

8   Groomsmen were required in the Middle Ages because many weddings required an actual **kidnapping** of the bride in order for the ceremony to take place. The groomsmen would steal the bride from other tribes or clans and bring her forcibly for the groom to marry. Another interpretation is that the groomsmen were recruited by the groom to help defend his bride from such kidnappings.

kidnapping *n.* 绑架，诱拐

White Gowns, Bouquets, and Veils

9   White wedding gowns became the **rage** during the reign of Queen Victoria of England, and white was thought to represent modesty and purity for the bride.

rage *n.* 流行

10   A wedding tradition as common as the white gown is the **bouquet**, carried today for aesthetic purposes. Originally, though, wedding bouquets included herbs such as **rosemary** and **lavender**, along with garlic, to **ward off** evil spirits and mask body odor. Orange blossoms were also popular, and represented fertility.

bouquet *n.* 花束
rosemary *n.* 迷迭香
lavender *n.* 薰衣草
ward off 驱除

11   Wedding veils were used by Roman and Greek brides as part of the arranged marriage process. Since most marriages were arranged for purposes of increasing a family's wealth or power, grooms were not allowed to see their brides until just prior to the marriage. The veils were used so the groom could not view the bride before the wedding and refuse to marry her if he did not like her looks. Another interpretation is that the veil helped **conceal** the bride so evil spirits would not know whom to curse.

conceal *v.* 隐藏

Something Old, Something New

⑫ The old saying "Something Old, Something New, Something Borrowed, Something Blue" is actually a superstition that started in medieval Europe as a means to **repel** evil spirits. Something old was a tie to your life prior to marriage. Something new represented the joining in marriage to a new spouse. Borrowing something from a currently wedded couple was thought to provide the new bride and groom good luck in their marriage. Something blue worn by the bride represented purity and **fidelity**.

repel *v.* 驱除

fidelity *n.* 忠诚

Tossing Rice and Tying the Knot

⑬ Tossing rice was a tradition started during pagan festivals as a wish for **bountiful** harvests. If the crops had been plentiful, grains such as wheat were thrown and if the crops had been bad, rice was thrown instead. The wedding guests also threw the rice to encourage high rates of fertility since it took many children to work the land.

bountiful *n.* 丰富的

⑭ Tying the knot refers to the ancient Roman custom of unmarried women wearing a **chastity girdle** closed with a series of knots. The groom would have to untie all the knots to **consummate** the marriage.

chastity *n.* 贞洁
girdle *n.* 腰带
consummate *v.* 完成

Doves and Weddings

⑮ Doves are meant to represent peace and new beginnings. Doves are thought to be used as a representation of the dove that flew from Noah's ark and came back after the flood. The dove held an olive branch that showed everything was not destroyed and in fact there was dry land and trees **sprouting** new life.

sprout *v.* 生长；产出

Extended Activities

Each of the following statements contains information given in one of the paragraphs in the passage. Identify the paragraph from which the information is derived and put the corresponding number in the space provided.

_____ 1) Originally, wedding bouquets included herbs such as rosemary and lavender, along with garlic, to ward off evil spirits and mask body odor.

_____ 2) Doves are thought to be used as a representation of the dove that flew from Noah's ark and came back after the flood.

_____ 3) Tossing rice was a tradition started during pagan festivals as a wish for bountiful harvests.

_____ 4) Wedding rings have most commonly been worn on the fourth finger of the left hand.

_____ 5) Borrowing something from a currently wedded couple was thought to provide the new bride and groom good luck in their marriage.

_____ 6) One explanation about groomsmen is that in the middle ages, the groomsmen would steal the bride from other tribes or clans and bring her forcibly for the groom to marry.

_____ 7) It is said that the veils were used so the groom could not view the bride before the wedding and refuse to marry her if he did not like her looks.

_____ 8) The bride was hit over the head with the cake to make her fertile.

_____ 9) The first rings were made of braided hemp and Romans later constructed their wedding rings of iron.

_____ 10) The wearing of a wedding ring on the fourth finger signifies the public proclamation of the union in the daylight.

Answer the following questions based on the understanding of the passage.

1) What are the symbolic meanings of wedding rings?

2) Why is the wedding ring worn on the fourth finger of the left hand?

3) Why is there a tradition of having groomsmen in the wedding ceremony?

4) Why is there a tradition for brides to wear wedding veils?

5) What does the saying "Something Old, Something New, Something Borrowed, Something Blue" mean?

Translate the following paragraph into English.

圣詹姆斯宫宣称，米德尔顿小姐将会佩戴婚戒，而威廉王子却不戴。夫妻双方通常在婚礼上交换婚戒，以表示对彼此的承诺。如果丈夫不戴婚戒又有什么关系呢？威廉王子的父亲戴了婚戒，他的祖父就没戴，他们的做法就无可非议。但人们对威廉王子不戴婚戒这事的反应却表明现在丈夫戴婚戒已成了一种定律。早在几个世纪以前，妻子戴婚戒就已成了理所当然的事，但丈夫戴婚戒的传统是"二战"时期才形成的。去国外打仗的男人们通常都戴着婚戒，这能让他们想起国内的妻子以及家庭。对于做手工工作的男人来说，戴婚戒可能会存在安全问题。但是威廉是如何解释的呢？一名皇室助手说，他不喜欢珠宝。

 # Exploring

Work in groups with your classmates to plan a future wedding in the western style for one of you and to act out the wedding ceremony. Your group work can be divided into the following steps.

Step 1 Search for more information about western wedding procedures and practices.

Step 2 Work out a wedding plan that includes the style of wedding dress, wedding rings, wedding vows, wedding procedures, and so on.

Step 3 Act out the scene of the wedding you have planned. The main characters are: bride, groom, bridesmaids, groomsmen, bride's father, priest and so on.

 # Mini-pedia

William and Catherine's Vows

Archbishop to Prince William: William Arthur Philip Louis, wilt thou have this woman to thy wedded wife, to live together according to God's law in the holy estate of matrimony? Wilt thou love her, comfort her, honour and keep her, in sickness and in health; and, forsaking all other, keep thee only unto her, so long as ye both shall live?

He answers: I will.

Archbishop to Catherine: Catherine Elizabeth, wilt thou have this man to thy wedded husband, to live together according to God's law in the holy estate of matrimony? Wilt thou love him, comfort him, honour and keep him, in sickness and in health; and, forsaking all other, keep thee only unto him, so long as ye both shall live?

She answers: I will.

The Archbishop receives Catherine from her father's hand. Taking Catherine's right hand, Prince William says after the Archbishop: I, William Arthur Philip Louis, take thee, Catherine Elizabeth to my wedded wife, to have and to hold from this day forward, for better, for worse: for richer, for poorer; in sickness and in health; to love and to cherish, till death us do part, according to God's holy law; and thereto I give thee my troth.

They loose hands. Catherine, taking Prince William by his right hand, says after the Archbishop: I, Catherine Elizabeth, take thee, William Arthur Philip Louis, to my wedded husband, to have and to hold from this day forward, for better, for worse: for richer, for poorer; in sickness and in health; to love and to cherish, till death us do part, according to God's holy law; and thereto I give thee my troth.

Prince William takes the ring and places it upon the fourth finger of Catherine's left hand. Prince William says after the Archbishop: With this ring I thee wed; with my body I thee honour; and all my worldly goods with thee I share: in the name of the Father, and of the Son, and of the Holy Ghost. Amen.

Reflection

Achievements	Yes	No
I am familiar with the practice and customs of a western wedding ceremony.		
I have understood cultural meanings of the practice and customs of a western wedding ceremony.		
I am aware of the differences in practice and customs between China and the U.K.		
I have acquired useful words and expressions related to weddings.		

LOUIS VUITTON

UNIT 9
FASHION

◆

GOALS

1 To understand the sociocultural significance of fashion trends;

2 To become aware of the development of western fashion brands;

3 To acquire useful words and expressions about fashion.

Warming-up

Answer the following questions:

1. Can you name some fashion brands? What are they?
2. What do you know about the brand Louis Vuitton?
3. Why do you think Louis Vuitton enjoys a world-famous reputation?

Reading

Passage One King Louis

By Robert Johnson

❶ Today it may be one of the biggest and most profitable luxury brands on the planet, a **byword** for **indulgence** from Beijing to Bond Street, but Louis Vuitton's origins are more humble, dating back to a young man who left home to make his living packing luggage for the great and the good in 19th-century Paris.

byword *n.* 代名词
indulgence *n.* 放纵；纵容

❷ Louis Vuitton himself was born the son of a miller in 1821 in Anchay, a **hamlet** in the Jura Mountains, not far from the Swiss border. The region was a poor one—**serfdom** had only been abolished less than 40 years previously, so Louis left to seek his fortune when he was a teenager, arriving in the French capital aged 16. This was the Paris of Victor Hugo's *Les Misérables*, with nearly one million **inhabitants**. As the composer Chopin said in a letter to a friend at the time, "Here you find the greatest luxury and the greatest filth, the greatest virtue and the greatest **vice**."

hamlet *n.* 小村庄
serfdom *n.* 农奴制

inhabitant *n.* 居民

vice *n.* 罪恶；堕落

❸   The teenager was taken on as an apprentice by Monsieur Maréchal, a box maker and packer on the Rue Saint-Honoré, then, as now, one of the main **thoroughfares** of fashionable Paris (today the achingly stylish store Colette sits on the site). Vuitton was to work there for 17 years. By the time he left the service of Maréchal, Charles-Louis Napoleon, the nephew of Napoleon Bonaparte, had **seized** power and had proclaimed himself Emperor Napoleon III. Paris was on the verge of becoming the global **epicentre** for taste and luxury and the city was a whirl of parties. The Emperor had employed Baron Haussmann to redesign the heart of the capital and create the city that we can see today. It was also the era of the enormous **crinoline** hooped skirt. These huge constructions were difficult to transport, so not surprisingly the services of professional packers were in great demand.

thoroughfare *n.* 大街

seize *v.* 抓住；夺取
epicentre *n.* 中心

crinoline *n.* 裙撑

❹   In 1854, Vuitton married the 17-year-old Clémence-Emilie Parriaux and decided to open his own company on the Rue des Capucines, just around the corner from his old boss. He advertised his services on a small poster that read, "Securely packs the most fragile objects. Specialising in packing fashions." He also decided to offer his clients trunks that he made himself in a workshop beside the recently opened Gare Saint-Lazare. His success was immediate.

❺   He became well known for his innovations, such as using **canvas** and glue for the casing rather than **hide**, which could **impregnate** the contents of the trunk with its smell. He also offered luggage in fashionable colours—in particular a pale shade he called Trianon grey.

canvas *n.* 帆布
hide *n.* 兽皮
impregnate *v.* 使吸收；浸渍

❻   But the big leap forward came in 1858 when he introduced the **slat** trunk, which was reinforced with beech slats and covered in Trianon grey canvas. This is arguably the first ever piece of modern luggage and is a design that is still used today. It was the dawn of the age of global travel and to keep up with booming demand, Vuitton moved his workshop to the village of Asnières on the banks of the Seine, three miles from central Paris, where

slat *n.* 板条

the company's luggage is still made. The factory also became the Vuitton family home, when Louis Vuitton built two villas in the grounds—one for himself and one for his son Georges, who took over the company on his father's death in 1892 and started the family business on its path of global expansion.

7 Georges had been sent to school in Jersey to learn English and had already opened the company's first overseas store in London, at 289 Oxford Street. Unfortunately, the years have not been as kind to central London as they have to Paris, and while Louis Vuitton's first place of work is now one of the world's **hippest** stores, the original London space is a branch of the Garfunkel's restaurant chain. Sales in the Oxford Street store were disappointing, so a few years later a new store opened on New Bond Street, opposite where the Maison Louis Vuitton can be found today.

hip *adj.* 时尚的

8 From here, the company went on to conquer the world. In 1889, the company presented a new canvas at the Exposition Universelle in Paris—where the Eiffel Tower was **unveiled**. The success of previous canvases, such as the Trianon grey, had led to an explosion of **counterfeits** so this new design included a **discreet** registered trademark and was patented—a very early example of fashion branding. The pattern of alternating brown and **beige** squares was known as Damier (French for chequerboard). It won a gold medal at the exposition and, since its reintroduction in 1996, has become synonymous with the label.

unveil *v.* 揭幕

counterfeit *n.* 赝品
discreet *adj.* 谨慎的
beige *n.* 米黄色

9 In 1890, the company patented a tumbler lock that was said to be **unpickable** and is still used today. Georges Vuitton publicly challenged the American escapologist Harry Houdini to try to crack it. "Sir, I believe the box you use in your act has been prepared for this purpose and I take the liberty of setting you a challenge. It involves escaping from a box of my own making, which will be closed, after you have gotten into it, by one of my staff."

unpickable *adj.* 无法撬开的

10 Houdini's response is not known.

11　The famous Monogram canvas was first introduced in 1896 then, in 1914, Vuitton opened the then biggest luggage store in the world on the Champs-Elysées, securing its reputation as the world's most luxurious travel brand—the favourite of **maharajahs**, millionaires and movie stars. And it could supply its customers with anything they could possibly need for their travels, from **intricate** vanity cases or trunks for polo mallets to the Secretary desk, complete with filing cabinets, collapsible desk and a typewriter. But if you preferred to travel light, in 1930, Louis Vuitton introduced the Keepall, the **prototype** of the modern holdall, which is still in production today.

maharajah *n.*（印度的）大
君，土邦主
intricate *adj.* 复杂的

prototype *n.* 原型

12　By the time the company reached its **centenary** in 1954, the Vuitton monogram was one of the most recognisable logos in the world. Salvador Dalí even took inspiration from it to create his own "Dalígram". Loyal customers included Georges Simenon, the Duke and Duchess of Windsor, Christian Dior, Hubert de Givenchy, Charles Aznavour, Luchino Visconti, Kirk Douglas... the list goes on. In 1959, the company introduced the supple monogrammed canvas coated in PVC that became its trademark.

centenary *n.* 百年纪念

13　Still a family firm, in 1984 the company was listed on the Paris Bourse. It already owned other luxury brands such as Givenchy, Veuve Clicquot and Loewe, and three years later it **merged** with the drinks giant Moët Hennessy to create what was to become the world's biggest luxury **conglomerate**, LVMH.

merge *v.* 合并
conglomerate *n.* 企业集团

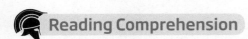 **Reading Comprehension**

14　**Decide whether the following statements are true or false. Write T for true and F for false.**

_____ 1) Louis Vuitton arrived in Paris at the age of 21.

_____ 2) Napoleon III employed Louis Vuitton to redesign Paris.

_____ 3) Louis Vuitton's success was immediate after he opened his own company.

_____ 4) A new store of LV was opened on New Bond Street because sales in the Oxford Street store were satisfactory.

_____ 5) The famous Monogram canvas was first introduced in 1896.

Answer the following questions based on the understanding of the passage.

1) Why were the services of professional packers in great demand?

2) What did Louis Vuitton use to make trunks?

3) What was the big leap of LV in 1858?

4) Why did Vuitton introduce a new design in 1889?

5) What products could Vuitton supply its customers with?

Put the following sentences in the right order according to the development of the Louis Vuitton company.

A. Vuitton opened the biggest luggage store in the world on the Champs-Elysées.

B. Louis Vuitton decided to open his own company.

C. The company introduced the Keepall.

D. The company introduced the supple monogrammed canvas coated in PVC.

E. Georges Vuitton overtook the business after his father's death.

F. The new design of the company won a gold medal at the Exposition Universelle.

G. The Damier pattern was reintroduced.

(　　) —— (　　) —— (　　) —— (　　) —— (　　) —— (　　) —— (　　)

🏛 Language in Use

Fill in the blanks with the words from the word bank. Change forms when necessary.

indulgence	alternate	achingly	innovate	leap
boom	emerge	conquer	unveil	discreet

1) He _____ out of his car and ran towards the house.

2) She _____ triumphant from the court after all the charges against her were dropped because of a lack of evidence.

3) All the pleasures and _____ of the weekend are over, and I must get down to some serious hard work.

4) Sung by the world's greatest tenor, this aria is _____ beautiful.

5) It may be many years before this dreadful disease is _____.

6) The fashion industry is always desperate to _____.

7) Private cars are banned from the city on _____ days.

8) They are very good assistants, very _____ —they wouldn't go talking to the press.

9) The insurance business suffered from a vicious cycle of _____ and bust.

10) The company recently _____ a test version of its new search engine.

Translate the following sentences into Chinese.

1) Here you find the greatest luxury and the greatest filth, the greatest virtue and the greatest vice.

2) Paris was on the verge of becoming the global epicentre for taste and luxury and the city was a whirl of parties.

3) He became well known for his innovations, such as using canvas and glue for the casing rather than hide, which could impregnate the contents of the trunk with its smell.

4) I believe the box you use in your act has been prepared for this purpose and I take the liberty of setting you a challenge. It involves escaping from a box of my own making, which will be closed, after you have gotten into it, by one of my staff.

5) Vuitton opened the then biggest luggage store in the world on the Champs-Elysées, securing its reputation as the world's most luxurious travel brand.

Oral Practice

Read the passage again and discuss with your partner about how Louis Vuitton became one of the world's biggest luxury brands and why it is still popular today.

Passage Two Why Did Men Stop Wearing High Heels?

By William Kremer

1 For generations they have signified femininity and **glamour**—but a pair of high heels was once an essential accessory for men.

glamour *n.* 魅力

2 Beautiful, **provocative**, sexy—high heels may be all these things and more, but even their most ardent fans wouldn't claim they were practical.

provocative *adj.* 刺激的；挑拨的

❸　They're no good for hiking or driving. They get stuck in things. Women in heels are advised to stay off the grass—and also ice, **cobbled** streets and posh floors.

cobbled *adj.* 铺鹅卵石的

❹　And high heels don't tend to be very comfortable. It is almost as though they just weren't designed for walking in.

❺　Originally, they weren't.

❻　"The high heel was worn for centuries throughout the near east as a form of riding footwear," says Elizabeth Semmelhack of the Bata Shoe Museum in Toronto.

❼　Good **horsemanship** was essential to the fighting styles of Persia—the historical name for modern-day Iran.

horsemanship *n.* 骑术

❽　"When the soldier stood up in his **stirrups**, the heel helped him to secure his **stance** so that he could shoot his bow and arrow more effectively," says Semmelhack.

stirrup *n.* 马镫
stance *n.* 站姿；立场

❾　At the end of the 16th century, Persia's Shah Abbas I had the largest cavalry in the world. He was keen to **forge** links with rulers in Western Europe to help him defeat his great enemy, the Ottoman Empire.

forge *v.* 铸造

❿　So in 1599, Abbas sent the first Persian **diplomatic** mission to Europe—it called on the courts of Russia, Germany and Spain.

diplomatic *adj.* 外交的

⓫　A wave of interest in all things Persian passed through Western Europe. Persian style shoes were enthusiastically adopted by **aristocrats**, who sought to give their appearance a virile, masculine **edge** that, it suddenly seemed, only heeled shoes could supply.

aristocrat *n.* 贵族
edge *n.* 优势

⓬　As the wearing of heels **filtered** into the lower ranks of society, the aristocracy responded by dramatically increasing the height of their shoes—and the high heel was born.

filter *v.* 过滤；渗透

⑬　In the muddy, **rutted** streets of 17th-century Europe, these new shoes had no utility value whatsoever—but that was the point.

rutted *adj.* 有车辙的

⑭　"One of the best ways that status can be conveyed is through impracticality," says Semmelhack, adding that the upper classes have always used impractical, uncomfortable and luxurious clothing to announce their privileged status.

⑮　"They aren't in the fields working and they don't have to walk far."

⑯　When it comes to history's most notable shoe collectors, the Imelda Marcos of his day was arguably Louis XIV of France. For a great king, he was rather **diminutively** proportioned at only 5 ft 4 in (1.63 m).

diminutively *adv.* 仅仅地

⑰　He supplemented his **stature** by a further 4 in (10 cm) with heels, often elaborately decorated with depictions of battle scenes.

stature *n.* 身高，身材

⑱　The heels and **soles** were always red—the dye was expensive and carried a martial **overtone**. The fashion soon spread overseas—Charles II of England's coronation portrait of 1661 features him wearing a pair of enormous red, French style heels—although he was over 6 ft (1.85 m) to begin with.

sole *n.* 鞋底
overtone *n.* 暗示，寓意

⑲　In the 1670s, Louis XIV issued an **edict** that only members of his court were allowed to wear red heels. In theory, all anyone in French society had to do to check whether someone was in favour with the king was to glance downwards. In practice, unauthorised, imitation heels were available.

edict *n.* 法令

⑳　Although Europeans were first attracted to heels because the Persian connection gave them a **macho** air, a craze in women's fashion for adopting elements of men's dress meant their use soon spread to women and children.

macho *adj.* 有男子气概的

㉑ "In the 1630s you had women cutting their hair, adding **epaulettes** to their outfits," says Semmelhack.

epaulette *n.* 肩章

㉒ "They would smoke pipes, they would wear hats that were very masculine. And this is why women adopted the heel—it was in an effort to masculinise their outfits."

㉓ From that time, Europe's upper classes followed a unisex shoe fashion until the end of the 17th century, when things began to change again.

㉔ "You start seeing a change in the heel at this point," says Helen Persson, a curator at the Victoria and Albert Museum in London. "Men started to have a squarer, more robust, lower heel, while women's heels became more slender, more **curvaceous**."

curvaceous *adj.* 曲线美的

㉕ The toes of women's shoes were often **tapered** so that when the tips appeared from her skirts, the wearer's feet appeared to be small and **dainty**.

taper *v.* 逐渐变细

dainty *adj.* 娇美的，俊俏的

㉖ Fast forward a few more years and the intellectual movement that came to be known as the Enlightenment brought with it a new respect for the rational and useful and an emphasis on education rather than privilege. Men's fashion shifted towards more practical clothing. In England, aristocrats began to wear simplified clothes that were linked to their work—managing country estates.

㉗ It was the beginning of what has been called the Great Male **Renunciation**, which would see men abandon the wearing of jewellery, bright colours and **ostentatious** fabrics in favour of a dark, more sober, and homogeneous look. Men's clothing no longer operated so clearly as a signifier of social class, but while these boundaries were being blurred, the differences between the sexes became more **pronounced**.

renunciation *n.* 放弃
ostentatious *adj.* 显眼的；卖弄的

pronounced *adj.* 显著的

㉘ "There begins a discussion about how men, regardless

of station, of birth, if educated could become citizens," says Semmelhack.

29 "Women, in contrast, were seen as emotional, sentimental and uneducable. Female desirability begins to be constructed in terms of **irrational** fashion and the high heel—once separated from its original function of horseback riding—becomes a primary example of impractical dress."

irrational *adj.* 不理性的，荒谬的

30 High heels were seen as foolish and **effeminate**. By 1740 men had stopped wearing them altogether.

effeminate *adj.* 柔弱的；女子气的

31 But it was only 50 years before they disappeared from women's feet too, falling out of favour after the French Revolution.

32 By the time the heel came back into fashion, in the mid-19th century, photography was transforming the way that fashions—and the female self-image—were constructed.

33 The 1960s saw a return of low heeled cowboy boots for men and some dandies **strutted** their stuff in platform shoes in the 1970s.

strut *v.* 炫耀

34 But the era of men walking around on their toes seems to be behind us. Could we ever return to an era of guys **squeezing** their big hairy feet into four-inch, shiny, brightly coloured high heels?

squeeze *v.* 挤，把……硬塞进

35 "Absolutely," says Semmelhack. There is no reason, she believes, why the high heel cannot continue to be **ascribed** new meanings—although we may have to wait for true gender equality first.

ascribe *v.* 归功于

36 "If it becomes a **signifier** of actual power, then men will be as willing to wear it as women."

signifier *n.* 符号，标记

Extended Activities

Each of the following statements contains information given in one of the paragraphs in the passage. Identify the paragraph from which the information is derived and put the corresponding number in the space provided.

_____ 1) The heels helped Persian soldiers to shoot more effectively on horseback.

_____ 2) Heels began to be worn by the lower classes in society.

_____ 3) Impracticality is a way to demonstrate privilege.

_____ 4) Charles II of England wore a pair of red heels in his coronation portrait.

_____ 5) Only members in the court of Louis XIV were allowed to wear red heels.

_____ 6) A unisex shoe fashion was followed by Europe's upper classes until the end of the 17th century.

_____ 7) English aristocrats began to wear simplified clothes.

_____ 8) High heels were regarded as effeminate.

_____ 9) High heels fell out of favor after the French Revolution.

_____ 10) New meanings might be ascribed to high heels.

Answer the following questions based on the understanding of the passage.

1) Why did European aristocrats adopt heels in the first place?

2) Why did the aristocrats increase the height of their shoes?

3) How did the heel change at the end of the 17th century?

4) What did the Great Male Renunciation involve?

5) Why might men start wearing high heels again?

Translate the following paragraph into English.

男性穿高跟鞋的风气从 18 世纪晚期之后就不再盛行了。但文化规范要求女性穿高跟鞋以使自己看起来更专业，一些男性认为这一点并不存在问题。在他们眼中，高跟鞋完全不会妨碍走路，而且穿脱都很方便。然而女性宣称穿高跟鞋走路很难受，而且长时间穿高跟鞋会对关节和血管产生副作用。在 21 世纪，异性恋男性在"穿着她的鞋走一英里"（A Mile in Her Shoes）这类抗议游行中穿高跟鞋是为社会所接受的。在这场游行中，多为异性恋白人的男性穿着红色的高跟鞋走一英里，对家庭暴力表示抗议。但通过在短时间内穿着高跟鞋，并且故意装作自己不知道如何穿高跟鞋走路，男性实际上强化了只有女性才可以穿高跟鞋的刻板印象。

Exploring

Work in groups to give a presentation on fashion styles around the world in history. Your group work can be divided into the following steps.

Step 1　Search for more information about fashion styles in different periods and countries.

Step 2　Select two to three fashion styles. Collect relevant information and analyze it.

Step 3　Give your presentation. Explain the characteristics of the fashion styles and the social meanings embedded in them.

Step 4　If possible, you could dress in the styles discussed in your presentation and put on a mini fashion show.

Mini-pedia

Fashion Week by the Numbers: Facts and Figures from New York to Paris

With the Spring/Summer 2016 shows behind us, we look back at some of the most impressive and surprising facts and figures to come out of New York, London, Milan and Paris this season.

72 years since the first ever New York Fashion Week

The first New York Fashion Week was held in 1943, and back then, was simply referred to as "Press Week." Paris hosted its first Fashion Week in 1945, while Milan started hosting Fashion Week in 1958. The first London Fashion Week took place in 1984.

62 editions of London Fashion Week

There have been 62 editions of London Fashion Week to date. Although the first London Fashion Week took place in 1984, this spring/summer showcase in September 2015

was the first time it was moved to a new location: the Brewer Street Car Park.

28 days of Fashion Month

Fashion "month" kicks off at New York Fashion Week on September 10 and ends in Paris on October 7. London Fashion Week runs September 18–22, while Milan Fashion Week is September 23–29.

$39 Billion contributed to the U.K. economy

According to London Fashion Week figures, the British fashion industry directly contributed $39 billion (£26 billion) to the U.K. economy this year. There are 797,000 jobs supported by the U.K. fashion industry as of 2014, and 158,000 new jobs expected to be created by the fashion industry by 2019.

350,800 times the #LFW hashtag was used on Twitter

There were also 2.5 million impressions on the @LondonFashionWeek twitter handle, while 121,000 images were tagged with #LFW on Instagram.

1.25 million Tweets about New York Fashion Week

New York Fashion Week was mentioned 1.25 million times on Twitter. Of the designers showcasing at New York Fashion Week, Michael Kors is the one that was most mentioned, with his name and Twitter handle being mentioned 113,000 times.

4% increase of models of color per season at NFW

This season, there were 28.4% models of color at New York Fashion Week. The season prior to this, there were 24.4%, and the season before that, just 20.9%.

 ## Reflection

Achievements	Yes	No
I have understood the sociocultural significance of fashion trends.		
I am aware of the development of western fashion brands.		
I have acquired useful words and expressions related to fashion.		

UNIT 10
CUISINE

◆

GOALS

1. To know about the culture and history of western cuisine;

2. To become aware of the differences in dieting habits between Chinese and Westerners;

3. To acquire some words and expressions about cuisine;

4. To grasp words describing trend.

Warming-up

Answer the following questions:

1. What does the old saying "Eating is Always Taken as the First Priority" mean?
2. Can you list some examples of American or British cuisine?
3. What do you know about the differences in dieting habits between Chinese and westerners?

Reading

Passage One **How Fast Food Has Changed Our Nation?**

❶ In order to regain control of our health, we need to let go of our childish attachments to food. I don't mean we are behaving like **petulant** children who want what they want when they want it. Rather, I mean we have become attached to the food of children.

petulant *adj.* 任性的

❷ While hamburgers were introduced to the United States in the early 20th century, the first fast-food restaurant chain, White Castle, opened its doors in 1921 in Wichita, Kansas selling burgers for a **nickel** along with side orders of fries and a cola. White Castle thrived, but it wasn't until after World War II that we began the journey to becoming a fast-food nation.

nickel *n.* 五美分

❸ The McDonald brothers designed their fast-food hamburger restaurant in an attempt to **streamline** the process of making food and to reduce the costs of production. Their **octagonal-shaped**

streamline *v.* 简化
octagonal-shaped *adj.* 八角形的

restaurant, which opened in San Bernardino, California, in 1945, also eliminated the need for waitresses, thus reducing operating costs even further. By 1951, McDonald's grossed $275,000, an unheard of amount of money for any small restaurant at the time.

❹ The decision to **franchise** their idea along with a distinctive architectural design (the Golden Arches) put McDonald's on the map. By 1960, there were 100 franchises operating across the country. But it was Ray Kroc, an equipment salesman who serviced McDonald's, who bought the business from the McDonalds's and took it to new levels of success.

franchise *v.* 特许经营

❺ Along with other pioneers in the fast-food businesses, including Burger King, and Wendy's, and numerous other Johnny-come-latelies to the scene, by 1990 fast food had taken over the American landscape with 11,800 McDonald's, 6,298 Burger Kings and 3,721 Wendy's.

❻ Today, more than 160,000 fast-food restaurants feed more than 50 million Americans each and every day, generating sales of more than $110 billion dollars annually.

❼ What do all these statistics, facts, and figures mean to us? It is no **coincidence** that the decline of our health has moved in direct proportion to the rise in the consumption of fast food. Forsaking home-cooked meals for snacks and fast food has more Americans than ever gorging on calorie-rich, nutrient-poor foods, sodas, and sweets. Over the last 25 years, we have come to take more of our calories from burgers, fries, pizza, and sweets than we have from home-cooked meals.

coincidence *n.* 巧合

❽ U.S. government surveys from 1977–1978, 1989–1991, and 1994–1996 reveal an alarming trend: More and more Americans ate their daily foods in the form of snack foods and fast food with each **subsequent** survey. The surveys also showed that Americans have come to prefer snacks to sit-down meals, and quick, easy, calorically dense treats like pizza, potato chips, and cookies to real food. Among 19–39-year-olds, restaurant and fast-food consumption has

subsequent *adj.* 随后的

more than doubled since the 1970s. In one study, Dr. Ashima Kant of City University of New York found that "energy-dense, nutrient-poor foods now account for more than 30% of American children's energy (calorie) intake."

9 On any given day, more than a quarter of all Americans will eat at a fast-food restaurant. This industry has, in a relatively short period of time, transformed not only the way we eat, but also our economy as well as the cultural landscape.

10 With fast-food restaurants everywhere, from airports to hospital lobbies, Americans are spending more on these foods than they do on higher education, computers, or new cars combined! A generation ago, more than three-quarters of the money spent on food was spent on **ingredients** to cook at home. Today more than half of money spent on food is spent on food eaten outside the home.

ingredient *n.* 原料，成分

11 McDonald's opens new restaurants at a rate of 2,000 per year and employs more people than any other organization, public or private. It is the largest purchaser of beef, pork, and potatoes and is the largest owner of retail property in the world. Via monster advertising campaigns that leave no **demographics** untouched, it has become the most famous brand in the world with the Golden Arches more recognized than the Christian cross, according to Eric Schlosser, author of *Fast Food Nation*.

demographics *n.* 人口统计

12 The fast-food industry is the largest employer of minimum-wage workers in the country, with migrant farm workers being the only group of people paid less. With the food prepared in enormous central kitchens and flavors coming from chemical plants along the New Jersey Turnpike, fast-food empires stand on top of huge industrial complexes that have destroyed the family farm, creating in its place industrial farms with absentee corporate owners.

13 The current **obesity epidemic** didn't just happen overnight. According to the National Bureau of Economic Research, the

obesity *n.* 肥胖
epidemic *n.* 流行病，传染病

generally persistent upward trend of Americans' weight began just after World War II. In the 1950s less than 10% of Americans were overweight or obese. As fast-food restaurants and processed foods took control of our diets, the numbers jumped. By 1975, (about the time McDonald's introduced the drive-through window,) the obesity rate in America had climbed to 15%. Since then, the overweight population has ballooned, with obesity rates topping 32%.

14   If the clear evidence of rising obesity isn't enough to scare you back to your own kitchen, consider the following statistics related to what have become known as "lifestyle" diseases: **diabetes** will kill twice as many women as breast cancer each year. Heart disease is the leading cause of death in both men and women, and has been for years. **Cardiovascular** disease kills more than 1 million people each year. That is 42% of all deaths. Not one state in the United States meets the Healthy People Guidelines of obesity at 15% or less. In 2010, only 1 state (Colorado) had an obesity rate of less than 20%. Nearly 34% of adult men and women over the age of 20 are obese. 2 out of 3 Americans are overweight (67%). In less than 10 years, a full 75% of adult Americans will be overweight. Childhood obesity has **tripled** in the past 30 years, to 25% of those less than 19 years of age. Americans consume more than 500 calories today than we did in the 1960s. $150 billion will be spent (and increase) each year on obesity-related illnesses. $174 billion (and increasing) will be spent each year on diabetes-related illnesses. In 2009, more than half the cancers diagnosed were cancers of the **prostate**, female breast, lung, and colon; a direct result of our high-fat diets, according to the National Research Council.

diabetes *n.* 糖尿病

cardiovascular *adj.* 心血管的

triple *v.* 增至三倍

prostate *n.* 前列腺

15   According to the National Cancer Institute, 75% of cancers are rooted in environmental and lifestyle causes—and can be prevented.

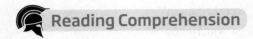

Reading Comprehension

① **Decide whether the following statements are true or false. Write T for true and F for false.**

_____ 1) Americans didn't begin the journey to becoming a fast-food nation until 1921.

_____ 2) The fast-food hamburger restaurant was originally designed in an attempt to streamline the process of making food and to reduce the costs of production.

_____ 3) The decline of our health has nothing to do with the rise in consumption of fast food.

_____ 4) Americans' weight began to increase just after the 1940s.

_____ 5) The author thinks highly of the development of fast-food restaurant chains.

② **Complete the sentences with the information from the passage.**

1) White Castle thrived, but it wasn't until _____ that we began the journey to becoming a fast-food nation.

2) The McDonald brothers designed their fast-food hamburger restaurant in an attempt to _____ and to reduce the costs of production.

3) In one study, Dr. Ashima Kant of City University of New York found that "_____ foods now account for more than 30% of American children's energy (calorie) intake."

4) The fast-food industry is the largest employer of minimum-wage workers in the country, with _____ being the only group of people paid less.

5) According to the National Cancer Institute, 75% of cancers are rooted in _____ —and can be prevented.

③ **Match the information of Column A with that of Column B.**

Column A	Column B
1) cardiovascular disease	a. will kill twice as many women as breast cancer each year
2) childhood obesity	b. is the leading cause of death in both men and women
3) diabetes	c. kills more than 1 million people each year
4) $150 billion	d. has tripled in the past 30 years
5) heart disease	e. will be spent each year on obesity-related illnesses
6) $174 billion	f. will be spent each year on diabetes-related illnesses

Language in Use

4 **Fill in the blanks with the words from the word bank. Make changes when necessary.**

> survey   obesity   subsequent   coincidence   landscape
> petulant   franchise   streamline   eliminate   epidemic

1) The young lady was standing on the deck to appreciate the beauty of the Three Gorges _____.

2) In a _____ carried out in 1987, 75% of the population identified themselves as middle class.

3) Windows is one of the _____ brands and products for Microsoft.

4) _____ people are advised to change their diet.

5) It is critical that the interests of these countries _____ with that of the invader.

6) An _____ broke out among children at the turning point of spring and summer.

7) How to _____ and prohibit drug abuse has become an international concern.

8) Some teachers will be interviewed in the _____ symposium.

9) As a college student, you cannot be as _____ as a little child.

10) All the staff are making efforts to _____ the production process to increase the output.

5 **Translate the following paragraph into Chinese.**

What do all these statistics, facts, and figures mean to us? It is no coincidence that the decline of our health has moved in direct proportion to the rise in the consumption of fast food. Forsaking home-cooked meals for snacks and fast food has more Americans than ever gorging on calorie-rich, nutrient-poor foods, sodas, and sweets. Over the last 25 years, we have come to take more of our calories from burgers, fries, pizza, and sweets than we have from home-cooked meals.

 Oral Practice

6 **Work in groups to discuss the question below and then each group is required to make a presentation by turns: What are the pros and cons of fast food? What do you think of having fast food in your daily diet?**

Passage Two British Cuisine

1　Yes, we do have a wide and varied **cuisine** in Britain today, no more do we suffer under the image of grey boiled meat! After years of **disparagement** by various countries (especially the French) Britain now has an **enviable culinary** reputation. In fact some of the great **chefs** now come from Britain, I kid you not!

cuisine n. 美食；烹饪

disparagement n. 轻蔑，轻视
enviable adj. 值得羡慕的
culinary adj. 烹饪的
chef n. 大厨

2　However Britain's culinary expertise is not new! In the past British cooking was amongst the best in the world. Mrs. Beeton is still one of the renowned writers of cookery books; her creations have now gained international popularity, years after her death.

3　Traditional British cuisine is substantial, yet simple and wholesome. We have long believed in four meals a day. Our fare has been influenced by the traditions and tastes from different parts of the British Empire: teas from **Ceylon** and **chutney**, **kedgeree**, and **mulligatawny soup** from India.

Ceylon n. 锡兰
chutney n. 酸辣酱
kedgeree n. 鸡蛋葱豆饭
mulligatawny soup 咖喱肉汤

A Brief History

4　British cuisine has always been multicultural, a potpourri of eclectic styles. In ancient times influenced by the Romans and in medieval times the French. When the Frankish Normans invaded, they brought with them the spices of the east: **cinnamon**, **saffron**, **mace**, **nutmeg**, pepper, and **ginger**. Sugar came to England at that time and was considered a spice—rare and expensive. Before the arrival of cane sugars, honey and fruit juices were the only sweeteners. The few Medieval cookery books that remain record dishes that use every spice in the larder, and chefs across Europe saw their task to be the almost alchemical transformation of raw ingredients into something entirely new (for centuries the English aristocracy ate French food) which they felt distinguished them from the peasants.

cinnamon n. 肉桂
saffron n. 藏红花
mace n. 肉豆蔻粉
nutmeg n. 肉豆蔻
ginger n. 姜

5　During Victorian times good old British **stodge** mixed with

stodge n. 乏味的食物

exotic spices from all over the Empire. And today despite being part of Europe we've kept up our links with the countries of the former British Empire, now united under the Commonwealth.

exotic adj. 外来的

6　One of the benefits of having an empire is that we did learn quite a bit from the colonies. From East Asia (China) we adopted tea (and exported the habit to India), and from India we adopted curry-style spicing. We even developed a line of spicy sauces including ketchup, **mint sauce**, Worcestershire sauce and deviled sauce to indulge these tastes. Today it would be fair to say that curry has become a national dish.

mint sauce 薄荷酱

7　Among English cakes and pastries, many are tied to the various religious holidays of the year. Hot Cross Buns are eaten on Good Friday, Simnel Cake is for Mothering Sunday, Plum Pudding for Christmas, and Twelfth Night Cake for Epiphany.

8　Unfortunately a great deal of damage was done to British cuisine during the two world wars. Britain is an island and supplies of many goods became short. The war effort used up goods and services and so less were left over for private people to consume. Ships importing food stuffs had to travel **in convoys** and so they could make fewer journeys. During the World War II food **rationing** began in January 1940 and was lifted only gradually after the war.

in convoy 结伴而行

rationing n. 定量配给

9　The British tradition of stews, pies and breads, according to the taste buds of the rest of the world, went into terminal decline. What was best in England was only that which showed the influence of France, and so English food let itself become a **gastronomic** joke and the French art of Nouvell Cuisine was adopted.

gastronomic adj. 烹饪学的

British Cuisine Today

10　In the late 1980s, British cuisine started to look for a new direction. **Disenchanted** with the overblown (and under-nourished) Nouvelle Cuisine, chefs began to look a little closer to home for

disenchanted adj. 不再着迷的

inspiration. Calling on a rich (and largely ignored) tradition, and **utilizing** many diverse and interesting ingredients, the basis was formed for what is now known as modern British food. **Game** has enjoyed a **resurgence** in popularity although it always had a central role in the British diet, which reflects both the abundant richness of the forests and streams and an old aristocratic prejudice against butchered meats.

utilize *v.* 利用

game *n.* 野味

resurgence *n.* 复活；再现

⑪　In London especially, one cannot only experiment with the best of British, but the best of the world as there are many distinct ethnic cuisines to sample, Chinese, Indian, Italian and Greek restaurants are amongst the most popular.

⑫　Although some traditional dishes such as roast beef and Yorkshire pudding, Cornish pasties, steak and kidney pie, bread and butter pudding, treacle tart, spotted dick or fish and chips, remain popular, there has been a significant shift in eating habits in Britain. Rice and pasta have accounted for the decrease in potato consumption and the consumption of meat has also fallen. Vegetable and salad oils have largely replaced the use of butter.

⑬　Roast beef is still the national culinary pride. It is called a "joint", and is served at midday on Sunday with roasted potatoes, Yorkshire pudding, two vegetables, a good strong **horseradish**, **gravy**, and **mustard**.

horseradish *n.* 辣根（调味品）

gravy *n.* 肉汁

mustard *n.* 芥末

⑭　Today there is more emphasis on fine, fresh ingredients in the better restaurants and markets in the U.K. offer food items from all over the world. Salmon, Dover sole, exotic fruit, Norwegian prawns and New Zealand lamb are choice items. Wild fowl and game are other specialties on offer.

⑮　In fact fish is still important to the English diet; we are after all an island surrounded by some of the richest fishing areas of the world. Many species swim in the cold offshore waters: sole, haddock, hake, plaice, cod (the most popular choice for fish and chips), turbot, halibut, mullet and John Dory. Oily fishes also abound (mackerel, pilchards, and herring) as do crustaceans like lobster and oysters. Eel, also common, is cooked into a wonderful pie with lemon, **parsley**, and **shallots**, all topped with **puff pastry**.

parsley *n.* 西芹

shallot *n.* 大葱

puff pastry 松饼

 Extended Activities

Each of the following statements contains information given in one of the paragraphs in the passage. Identify the paragraph from which the information is derived and put the corresponding number in the space provided.

_____ 1) People can experiment with the best of British as well as the best of the world as there are many distinct ethnic cuisines to sample.

_____ 2) Different cakes and pastries are eaten on various religious holidays in Britain.

_____ 3) Game enjoyed a resurgence in popularity when British cuisine started to look for a new direction in the late 1980s.

_____ 4) British food, which used to be despised by various countries (especially the French), now has an enviable culinary reputation.

_____ 5) Fish is still important to the English diet as there are some rich fishing areas in Britain.

_____ 6) British cuisine was greatly damaged during the two world wars.

_____ 7) There has been a significant shift in eating habits in Britain although some traditional dishes remain popular.

_____ 8) British fare has been influenced by the traditions and tastes from different parts of the British Empire.

_____ 9) When the Frankish Normans invaded, sugar came to England and was considered a spice.

_____ 10) Roast beef is served at midday on Sunday.

Answer the following questions based on the understanding of the passage.

1) What impression does British food leave on the whole world?

2) What did British food learn from British colonies?

3) Can you list some examples to show how English cakes and pastries are tied to religious holidays?

4) What changes took place in British cuisine in the late 1980s?

5) What role does fish play in the English diet?

Translate the following paragraph into English.

研究者发现，三分之一的人在大多数就餐时间都会选择比萨饼和意大利肉酱粉。投票的成年人中，四分之一以上将意大利菜列为最喜爱的菜肴。然而，并非所有的经典英国菜都消亡了——烤肉大餐和烤土豆然仍受到坚定地追捧。这项 2000 人参加的研究结果表明：有百分之八十二的人认为，传统英国菜正从我们的餐桌上消失，超过四分之一的人说他们没有时间准备一顿地道的英国菜，另有四分之一的人就是喜欢吃外国菜，但是还有四分之三的人认为我们应该尽量烹饪传统菜肴。

 # Exploring

Design a daily diet for yourself and give reasons. Your work should include the following points.

- the dishes for three meals in details
- give reasons for your design

 # Mini-pedia

Seven Traditional British Dishes That Have (Somehow) Stood the Test of Time

When you think of British food it's usually pork pies, bangers 'n' mash and fish and chips that come to mind. While these are popular and traditional British dishes, there are others that are far more interesting, historical or downright weird.

You should definitely give these seven British foods a try while you live in the U.K.

1. Bubble and squeak

This dish dates back as far as 1806 and consists of shallow-fried vegetables leftover from a roast dinner. It could include potato, Brussels sprouts, carrots, peas, cabbage or any other remaining vegetables.

2. Jellied eels

These are bits of eel in fish-flavoured jelly with malt vinegar on top. In the 18th century the Thames was so polluted and foul that the only fish that could survive in it was the eel. This led to many eel-based recipes being devised by London's poor communities.

3. Black pudding

Black pudding is a type of sausage made from pork blood, meat and/or fat, and bread or oatmeal. It can be fried, baked, grilled or boiled and eaten hot or cold.

4. Scotch eggs

Scotch eggs are a popular picnic food consisting of a boiled egg wrapped in pork sausage meat, encased in breadcrumbs and deep fried or baked.

5. The Bedfordshire Clanger

The Bedfordshire Clanger is a main meal and dessert in one. This sweet and savoury dish originated in the county of Bedfordshire and is essentially an elongated suet pudding.

6. Haggis

Haggis is a savoury pudding made from a sheep's heart, liver and lungs. The organs are minced with onion, oatmeal, suet and spices and encased in the animal's stomach or (nowadays) an artificial casing.

7. Stargazy pie

The Stargazy pie is a true oddity. This pilchard, potato and egg filled pastry comes complete with an arrangement of fish heads that poke up through the crust as if gazing at the stars.

 # Reflection

Achievements	Yes	No
I am familiar with the dieting habits of western countries.		
I have understood the culture and history of western cuisine.		
I am aware of the differences in dieting habits between Chinese and westerners.		
I have acquired useful words and expressions related to cuisine.		

UNIT 11
SPORTS

◆

GOALS

1. To familiarize with the history of sports in the world;
2. To understand some issues about the Olympic Games in Rio 2016;
3. To become aware of the benefits of doing sports;
4. To acquire useful words and expressions related to sports.

Warming-up

Answer the following questions:

1. Do you know the reason why ancient Greece is called the cradle of sports?
2. What do you know about the Olympic Games in Rio 2016?

Reading

Passage One History of World Sports

By Robert Edelman and Wayne Wilson

① Sports is a modern set of practices closely tied to the rapid evolution of capitalism and the growth of cities. The Industrial Revolution had its roots in the **revamping** of agriculture and exploitation of colonial people and goods from expires. Nevertheless, physical contests of all sorts had existed for centuries prior to the **modernity**, and we cannot ignore them. Those who have argued ancient Greece was the cradle of democracy and civilization also see it as a matching cradle of sport. The practice and organization of physical contests were highly developed and well organized in the Greek and Roman empires. From the Olympic Games to the spectacles of **gladiatorial** combat, the ancient world has often been seen as the first site of sporting activity. In both places sport became a form of popular culture through which citizens were created. The **fit** athletes and the fit warrior became central figures in the **projection** and maintenance of empire.

revamp *v.* 修改

modernity *n.* 现代性

gladiatorial *adj.* 争论的

fit *adj.* 强壮的
projection *n.* 预测；规划；
设计

②   By the 19th century, philo-Hellenism became a driving force in the creation of the modern Olympics. The founder of the modern version of the Olympic Games, Baron Pierre de Coubertin, claimed to be reviving the games of ancient Greece, but he also used the Greek example to gain support in Germany and other countries for his movement. One must then ask if this highly male, elitist, and positive interpretation of these ancient societies was connected to only one of many possible interpretations of the classical world. If ancient Greece, in particular, was the cradle of civilization, what sort of civilization was it, and what role did sport play in its creation and reproduction?

③   It has been said that medieval sport is still awaiting its H. A. Harris, the author of one of definitive texts on ancient Greek sport. Nevertheless, there is a body of literature on medieval sport, **albeit** one that heavily on British and western European sources from the later Middle Ages. Many sports of the period such as **wrestling**, **archery**, and water tilting had martial origins. One study of the sporting pursuits of 13th-century English peasants noted that nearly half were "war-related". People at both ends of the social **spectrum** pursued sport, while religious leaders attempted to exert varying degrees of control over these bodily and often violent pastimes. The tournament, in which noblemen engaged in **jousts** and **melees**, is the best-known form of medieval sport, but less violent activities such as forms of tennis also took root. One of the differences between medieval and modern sport is the increased degree to which contemporary sport seeks to minimize violence, injury, and death and thus be less warlike. Sport, as Norbert Elias wrote, is part of the "civilizing process", but battles on the playing field are **mimetic** and not real despite the militarized language that often surrounds them.

④   The early modern period witnessed the rise of several activities that adopted some of the defining characteristics of modern sport. This process occurred in only some sports and was advanced at different rates in different countries. Cricket, horse racing, and golf, to cite three examples of sport that eventually

albeit *conj.* 虽然；即使

wrestling *n.* 摔跤
archery *n.* 剑术

spectrum *n.* 系列；范围

joust *n.*（骑士）骑着马用长矛打斗
melee *n.* 混战；格斗

mimetic *adj.* 模仿的

153

became global, developed written rules, formed clubs, recorded results, and consciously sought to attract spectators in the pre-modern period.

5 Originating in the 19th century, the modern Olympic Games are the world's premier sports event. Because of their magnitude and public visibility, the Olympics have provided a stage on which most of the major developments and conflicts of modern sport have played out for more than one hundred years. The International Olympic Committee, which drew its early inspiration from the gentleman amateurs of Victorian Britain, has confronted the major issues of the 20th century—nationalism, professionalism, and commercialism, not to mention war and peace. Initially, banning female participation, the Olympics became one of the principle **arenas** where women struggled for inclusion. Scholarly interest has been **piqued** by the widespread perception, encouraged by the IOC, that Olympic sport is a "movement" capable of inspiring social and political transformations. Along with a politically liberal belief in the possibility of social improvement. In practice, **commitment** to these ideals was combined with continuing cooperation with some of world's **vilest regimes**. Accordingly, historians have been eager to analyze this **grandiose**, idealistic framing of the Olympic, frequently offering critical alternative readings of the Games and their meanings. In the course of the most recent wave of globalization, the Olympics have transformed from a festival of nominal amateurs to an **extravaganza** of openly professional athletes competing on a world stage promoted by global marketing and sponsorship campaigns.

arena *n.* 竞技场
pique *v.* 使愤恨；使恼怒

commitment *n.* 承诺，许诺
vile *adj.* 可耻的
regime *n.* 政权，政体
grandiose *adj.* 宏伟的；浮夸的

extravaganza *n.* 内容浮夸的作品；盛事

6 As a result, a high-stakes **cauldron** of competition has emerged that offers great monetary reward for the most visible and elite performers. Although doping in sport is often framed as a contemporary issue driven by athletes' desires to win riches, athletes ancient and modern, have long sought to supplement their normal diets with food, drinks, or drugs to improve sport performance. Accounts of 19th-century sport doping abound. The IOC discussed the problem as early as the 1930s. In the post-

cauldron *n.* 大锅

World War II period, the use of performance-enhancing drugs grew throughout the world. In 1968 the IOC introduced drug testing, and most other major sports organizations eventually followed. Efforts at doping control in the late 20th century were carried out by **disparate** organizations with almost no coordination among them. A series of international doping scandals in the 1990s **culminated** in the creation of the World Anti-Doping Agency, which sought to impose a single anti-doping regime on world sport. The history of doping and anti-doping efforts raised fundamental questions about how different societies view the nature of sport, competition, fair play, as well as the health and rights of athletes. In an environment in which the **hormonal**, structural, and genetic manipulation of athletes are all possible, doping squarely raises the question of what it means to be human.

disparate *adj.* 完全不同的

culminate *v.* 达到极点

hormonal *adj.* 激素的；荷尔蒙的

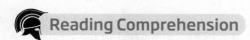

Reading Comprehension

① **Decide whether the following statements are true or false. Write T for true and F for false.**

_____ 1) Physical contests existed before the Industrial Revolution.

_____ 2) Greece was seen as the cradle of sports because of its democracy and civilization.

_____ 3) "War-related" activities such as wrestling, archery, as well as less violent ones such as tennis, took root in the Middle Ages.

_____ 4) The International Olympic Committee has confronted the major issues of the twentieth century—nationalism, professionalism, and commercialism, as well as war and peace.

_____ 5) The main purpose for the athletes to take drugs in the competition is to improve sport performance.

② **Complete the sentences with the information from the passage.**

1) Sports is a modern set of practices closely tied to the _____ and the growth of cities.

2) Many sports of the period such as wrestling, archery, and water tilting had martial origins. One study of the sporting pursuits of thirteenth-century English peasants noted that nearly half were _____.

3) One of the differences between medieval and modern sport is the increased degree to which contemporary sport seeks to _____ and thus be less warlike.

4) In the course of the most recent wave of globalization, the Olympics have transformed from a festival of nominal amateurs to an extravaganza of openly professional athletes competing on a world stage promoted by _____.

5) The history of doping and anti-doping efforts raised fundamental questions about _____, as well as the health and rights of athletes.

Put the following sentences in the right order according to the history of sports.

A. The Olympics became one of the principle arenas where women struggled for inclusion.

B. People at both ends of the social spectrum pursued sport, while religious leaders attempted to exert varying degrees of control over these bodily and often violent pastimes.

C. The practice and organization of physical contests were highly developed and well organized in the Greek and Roman empires.

D. A series of international doping scandals in the 1990s culminated in the creation of the World Anti-Doping Agency.

E. Cricket, horse racing, and golf, to cite three examples of sports that eventually became global.

F. Baron Pierre de Coubertin used the Greek example to gain support in Germany and other countries for his movement.

(   ) —— (   ) —— (   ) —— (   ) —— (   ) —— (   )

Language in Use

Fill in the blanks with the words or phrases from the word bank. Make changes when necessary.

evolution	cradle	confront	exert... over...	fit
play out	witness	along with	impose... on...	not to mention

1) Although America is said to be the _____ of beach volleyball, Brazil is still proud of this sport because of its beautiful beach scenery.

2) The Union's reform _____ against a background of rising unemployment.

3) China has greatly achieved in these 20 years, and it has got the quick development in politics, economy, _____ its culture.

4) He was too wise to be _____ by fair words spoken without sincerity.

5) Faced with the increasing pressures of daily life, we should take more physical activities to maintain _____.

6) It is well acknowledged that human beings are _____ from apes.

7) The _____ of this scandal has pulled the President off the center of rights.

8) How much influence can parents _____ their children in the era of Internet?

9) We have all _____ with a serious problem: to leave or to stay!

10) Mary, _____ her husband had immigrated into America due to the expansion of their overseas business.

5 **Translate the following paragraph into Chinese.**

Those who have argued ancient Greece was the cradle of democracy and civilization also see it as a matching cradle of sport. The practice and organization of physical contests were highly developed and well organized in the Greek and Roman empires. From the Olympic Games to the spectacles of gladiatorial combat, the ancient world has often been seen as the first site of sporting activity. In both places sport became a form of popular culture through which citizens were created. The fit athletes and the fit warrior became central figures in the projection and maintenance of empire.

Oral Practice

6 **Read the passage again and discuss with your partner about the key line in the history of sports. You may use the following expressions in your discussion.**

ancient Greek	violent	medieval	cradle of civilization	IOC
globalization	doping	war-related	the World Anti-Doping Agency	

Passage Two Reality in the Coming Rio Olympics

1 "Cariocas" (Rio natives) must be **having a ball**, you might think. They have sun, sea, football on the beach and now the

have a ball 玩耍，娱乐

honour of hosting the world's biggest sporting event... Rio becomes the first South American city to ever host the Olympic Games. These are the first games to be held in a Portuguese-speaking country, the first to be held entirely in the host country's winter, the first since 1968 to be held in Latin America, and the first since 2000 to be held in the Southern Hemisphere.

2　Officials in Rio de Janeiro hope hosting the 2016 Olympics would help make it a first-class city. And the 2016 Rio Olympics is supposed to be the second of a one-two **punch** announcing Brazil's arrival as a world power through dominance in sports. But their days are also filled with the loud noise and dust of construction work, so you can forgive them if they don't sound very enthusiastic about the Olympic Games at the moment. They know they will be putting up with a lot more roadworks and infrastructure building before the Olympic torch is lit in the Maracanã Stadium next 5th August.

punch *n.* 冲击；力量

3　Delays in **venue** construction and a **chaotic** appearance gave the International Olympic Committee (IOC) a **fright** in 2014. The Brazilian government has since cleaned up its act and was praised recently by the IOC for being "**on the right track**". But what might be more difficult to clean are the Rodrigo de Freitas Lagoon and Guanabara Bay. They, among others, will be venues for the sailing and rowing competitions. The problem is they are heavily polluted, which could be harmful to athletes. The issue is likely to be in the news headlines for a while. There have also been stories of corruption. But the authorities hope by the time the summer comes they'll be celebrating a scandal-free event.

venue *n.* 场所；地点
chaotic *adj.* 混沌的；混乱的
fright *n.* 恐吓，惊吓
on the right track 运转正常

4　Brazil has learnt a lot from hosting the World Cup last year. Some businesses realized they **missed a trick** by not being able to communicate properly with their international customers. This summer Brazilians will be trying out the English they've been learning and be ready to offer a good service before the first foreign sports enthusiasts stroll down the lively streets of Rio. Restaurants should realize that using the internet to translate the

miss a trick 丧失机会

menu literally is not a good idea: "bife a cavalo" isn't really "horse steak"—it's beef with a fried egg on top! And the **intriguingly** named "contrafilé", which means "against the file", is nothing more than a sirloin steak.

intriguingly *adv.* 有趣地

⑤ Security was a key challenge for Brazil when hosting the World Cup and it is no different for the Olympics. If London's police were concerned mainly about the possibility of terrorist attacks when the city hosted the games in 2012, Brazilian police will be working to prevent street crime. As with other developing countries, crime rates are high and there are too many guns around. Visitors are to **keep their wits about** them. Sometimes petty thieves with only quick hands for weapons try to relieve you of your belongings.

keep the wits about 时刻警惕

⑥ For those on a low budget and with a taste for adventure, there will be plenty of options for accommodation in the city's "favelas" or **shanty** towns. These do have a reputation for violent crime committed by drug gangs, as shown in the 2002 Brazilian film *City of God*. But some favelas have changed since a government policy called "pacification" was introduced in 2008. A number of business-minded favela residents will be welcoming tourists into their homes, which they've turned into guesthouses. Some favelas are on the city's steep mountainsides, so guests will be guaranteed **panoramic** views of Rio at least. And of the old-style favelas... well, *City of God*'s co-director Fernando Meirelles is part of the team planning the Olympics opening ceremony.

shanty *n.* 简陋的小屋

panoramic *adj.* 全景的，全貌的

⑦ So while Cariocas are already turning into athletes themselves—by jumping and running across construction sites on their daily trip to work—they know that the games might make for a great spectacle. Brazilians are warm and cheerful, and international visitors will have a good time in their company. Preparation for big events is stressful—Londoners were a bit pessimistic ahead of their Olympics. But while Brazilians might have their reservations, deep down, very deep down, they know something others don't. As an old local saying goes: "Deus é Brasileiro" (God is Brazilian). They hope he will give them a hand. And whatever else, Brazilians will show the world why they have such a reputation as party people!

 Extended Activities

Each of the following statements contains information given in one of the paragraphs in the passage. Identify the paragraph from which the information is derived and put the corresponding number in the space provided.

_____ 1) Brazil can learn a lot from hosting the World Cup.

_____ 2) Brazilians all have the confidence to treat the international visitors because they are warm and cheerful.

_____ 3) It will make Brazilian police busy in preventing street crime.

_____ 4) It is the first time for the Olympic Games to be held in a Portuguese-speaking country.

_____ 5) Many business-minded favela residents will invite tourists into their homes, which they have turned into guesthouses.

_____ 6) Aside from the construction problem, corruption is another issue to be considered seriously.

_____ 7) The officials wish to make Rio a first-class city by hosting the 2016 Olympics.

Choose the correct answer to the following questions.

1) What makes people from Rio unhappy about hosting the Olympics?

   A. They've had enough of sport already—they already play football on the beach.

   B. The daily dust and noise coming from Olympics building sites disturbs people.

   C. Rio is the first South American city to host the Olympic Games.

2) Which of these statements is true?

   A. The government has cleaned the Rodrigo de Freitas Lagoon at the request of the IOC.

   B. After complaints, the government built a racing track and the IOC was happy.

   C. The pollution in Guanabara Bay and the Rodrigo de Freitas Lagoon will continue attracting journalists' attention.

3) What should restaurant workers in Rio do to please customers?

   A. Lower the food price.

   B. Learn English to communicate better.

   C. Search for literal translations online.

4) What is a cause for concern in developing countries according to the passage?

    A. Quick hands.

    B. Crime rates.

    C. Overpopulation.

5) Which of these statements is correct?

    A. All the parts of favelas have beautiful views of Rio.

    B. Brazilians are sure that preparing for the Olympics will go smoothly.

    C. Londoners were concerned before putting on their Olympic Games in 2012.

 Translate the following paragraph into English.

第 31 界世界奥林匹克运动会，也称为 2016 里约夏季奥运会，于 2016 年 8 月 5 日至 21 日在巴西里约热内卢隆重举行。作为一项国际赛事，里约奥运会吸引了来自全世界 205 个国家的 11 000 多名运动员参加。其间，他们为 28 个赛事、306 枚奖牌展开激烈的争夺。橄榄球和高尔夫是自 2009 年以来新增的奥运比赛项目。然而巴西政局的不稳定让这次里约奥运会极具争议。国家的经济危机、寨卡病毒、瓜纳巴拉海湾的污染以及俄罗斯选手的兴奋剂事件更使此次奥运雪上加霜，影响了运动员参加比赛的积极性。

 # Exploring

Work in groups to discuss the Beijing Olympic Games in 2008. Your group work can be divided into the following steps.

Step 1   Search for more information about the Beijing Olympic Games in 2008.

Step 2   Work in groups and each group takes charge of one aspect of the information about the Beijing Olympic Games in 2008, such as the venue, the athletes, the media, the medals, etc.

Step 3   Give your presentation in class.

 # Mini-pedia

What Are the Ways Sports Improve the Quality of Life?

Quality of life is a phrase used to define people's sense of well-being. It's something that people aspire to have and, while it's not easy to quantify, you know when you have the quality of life that makes you feel good. Sport can make a significant contribution to your quality of life, and numerous academic studies show it can impact physical and mental health, social life and life opportunities.

The Exercise Effect

Western society faces a number of health issues that affect quality of life. These are primarily cardiovascular disease, obesity and diabetes. The U.S. Department of Health and Human Services states that exercise plays an important role in preventing these. Type II diabetes is associated with a sedentary lifestyle and obesity leads to an array of health problems, including an increased risk of stroke. A 2001 study by I. Thune and A.S. Furberg also shows that there is a possible link between lack of exercise and colon cancer.

Feeling Better in Yourself

A study by the Centers for Disease Control demonstrates the powerful effect sport and exercise can have on how you feel about your day-to-day life. The study's results are based on the recommended guideline of 30 minutes of moderate exercise daily on most days of the week, or 20 minutes of intense exercise on at least three days of the week. The study of 175,850 adults revealed that if you exercise according to the recommended guidelines, you'll have twice as many days when you feel physically and mentally healthy compared to a person who doesn't exercise.

Meet the Neighbors

Sport is about so much more than just getting exercise; it's an opportunity to meet people. Loneliness diminishes quality of life and U.K. research on the relationship between social interaction and health suggests that people with good social networks are happier and healthier, live longer and are at less risk of heart disease. The social benefit of sport also has a strong link with its benefits for mental health. Sport is considered to have an effect on depression, anxiety,

mood and self-esteem. In communities where there are political, racial or religious divisions, sport can bring people together and have a socially stabilizing effect.

Life Enhancer

Sport can enhance the quality of life of anyone who faces physical challenges. A study of athletes with cerebral palsy revealed that the majority of the athletes believed sport had a strong influence on quality of life, as well as family life, social life and physical health. Sport can have the same effect on people who are recovering from heart attacks and strokes or who have chronic health conditions that create a feeling of constant tiredness. It can also enhance the lives of people facing the challenges of aging, keeping them young at heart. It can help athletes come back from injury.

 # Reflection

Achievements	Yes	No
I am familiar with the history of sports in the world.		
I have understood some issues about the Olympic Games in Rio 2016.		
I am aware of the benefits of doing sports.		
I have acquired useful words and expressions related to sports.		

UNIT 12
OPERA

◇

GOALS

1. To know some general facts of western opera;
2. To learn the features of western opera;
3. To familiarize with certain opera composers and their works;
4. To obtain approaches to the appreciation of opera works.

Warming-up

Answer the following questions:

1. How much do you know about Mozart?
2. Have you ever watched an opera by Mozart?
3. Which opera work of Mozart impresses you most?

Reading

Passage One My Favourite Mozart Opera

❶　Take a **straw poll** of the world's favourite Mozart opera and I guess *Die Zauberflöte* or *Le Nozze di Figaro* would come out on top. But I think my vote would go to *Die Entführung aus dem Serail* (*The Abduction from the Seraglio*).

straw poll 民意测验

❷　I don't think it's the **supreme** masterpiece, but it has all the irresistible charm and beauty of youth—charged with a romantic vitality that must reflect some of the 25-year-old composer's own optimism, newly liberated from the court of the Archbishop of Salzburg.

supreme *adj.* 最高的

❸　First performed in Vienna in 1782, it quickly became a big success despite the celebrated (perhaps mythical) **verdict** of the Emperor Joseph II—"Too many notes, my dear Mozart!" Yet the implication that it is prolix has some substance: the score is one of great **intricacy** and brilliance, and there are moments when it

verdict *n.* 结论

intricacy *n.* 错综，复杂

seems to get carried away with itself.

④ Like *Die Zauberflöte* and most operas written in German in the late 18th century, its form is that of a Singspiel ("sung play"), containing passages of spoken dialogue between its musical numbers, rather in the fashion of a **Broadway** show.

Broadway *n.* 百老汇

⑤ Mozart suffered headaches as he wrote it: desperate for money, he needed to write something with immediate popular appeal, but he also yearned to write something freshly original too.

⑥ The libretto he **inherited** had to be both cut and expanded, and a combination of **obstinacy** and inexperience—youth again!— meant that the structure and balance remain skewed, with both the leading characters given one aria more than they strictly require.

inherit *v.* 继承
obstinacy *n.* 固执

⑦ But the choruses, duets and ensembles are marvels: if I had to pick one number that embodied its genius, it would be the astonishing **quartet** which concludes the second act, passing through a range of moods and emotions until it arrives at a **jubilant** climax.

quartet *n.* 四重奏
jubilant *adj.* 欢呼的

⑧ The story may be simple, but there are resonances which audiences today may find discomfiting. Konstanze, a German lady, has been seized off a boat and imprisoned in the palace of the Turkish Pasha Selim, who first tries to seduce her and then threatens torture if she does not join his harem. She resists **adamantly**. The lecherous Osmin is assigned to guard her and her pert English maid Blonde.

adamantly *adv.* 坚定无比地

⑨ Rescue is on the way in the shape of her Spanish lover Belmonte and his servant Pedrillo who gain access to the palace. But their attempts to escape Selim's clutches are foiled and the four Europeans are told to expect execution—until Selim recognises Belmonte as the son of a colonial governor who many years ago had robbed him of his property. He decides that he does not wish to follow in the moral footsteps of someone he so despises and, with airy contempt, he lets the **Christians** go free.

Christian *n.* 基督徒

⑩   The themes would have been familiar to 18th-century audiences. One must remember that tales of Christian women being seized and sold by Arab pirates were vividly in the news, making the situation less **farcical** than it appears nowadays. On the other hand, Montesquieu and Voltaire had made it a commonplace that Muslims could teach Christians a thing or two.

farcical *adj.* 滑稽的

⑪   So one mistake Mozart made was choosing to leave Selim as a spoken role: his ardour for Konstanze as well as his cruelty and his final change of heart make him potentially the opera's most interesting character, but without any music to **animate** him, he seems two-dimensional. Much more vivid is the portrayal of the vicious Buffoon Osmin in a crude racist caricature who nevertheless has irresistible comic **bravado**.

animate *v.* 使有生气

bravado *n.* 虚张声势

⑫   It is a coincidence that the opera's heroine has a name almost identical to that of Mozart's future wife, but one can only imagine that the ravishing sensuality in the former's music is in some sense dedicated to the latter, and that Mozart saw in himself something of Belmonte. His arias are imbued with grace—and because they lie high in the tenorial range and demand exceptional breath and pitch control, they are also difficult to sing.

⑬   Not as difficult, however, as Konstanze's, which demand such an exhausting variety of moods and techniques that very few of even the greatest **sopranos** have ever mastered the role—let alone relished it. Most daunting of all is the long number Martern aller Arten ("Tortures of All Kinds"), in which everything stops for nearly 10 minutes as Konstanze assures Selim in music of relentless virtuosity that she will not sacrifice her honour to him. Even Joan Sutherland and Edita Gruberová **dreaded** this one.

soprano *n.* 女高音

dread *v.* 惧怕

⑭   The difficulty of finding singers who can surmount these challenges means that *Entführung* is relatively seldom performed. In pre-war Britain, it had become a rarity, and it was only Glyndebourne's decision to play it over three **consecutive** seasons—1935 to 1937—that gave it a firmer footing in the repertory.

consecutive *adj.* 连贯的，连续的

⑮ But there have been few satisfactory productions anywhere in the post-war era, and too often the show comes out looking either picture-postcard, panto or po-faced. You can't take it too seriously, but you can't play it for laughs either.

⑯ A relatively straightforward staging by Giorgio Strehler at the Salzburg Festival in the seventies was much admired in its day, and a **freewheeling** version at Garsington last year directed by Daniel Slater, in which Selim became a Russian oligarch and Belmonte an American college jock, also worked surprisingly well. But Welsh National Opera, Scottish Opera and Opera North all **flopped** with their recent efforts, the Royal Opera hasn't **tackled** it for 15 years, ENO for more than 30.

freewheeling *adj.* 随心所欲的

flop *v.* 失败
tackle *v.* 解决

⑰ Glyndebourne has staged four productions since the war (the most visually memorable of them designed by Oliver Messel) and two of its Konstanzes, Margaret Price and Valerie Masterson, are still warmly recalled. But it's now nearly two decades since the opera was performed here, and one hopes that the return of this enchanting work next season, with an **intriguing** cast directed by David McVicar and conducted by Robin Ticciati, will bring it new life.

intriguing *adj.* 有趣的

Reading Comprehension

🏛 **Decide whether the following statements are true or false. Write T for true and F for false.**

_____ 1) Take a straw poll of the world's favourite Mozart opera and I guess *Die Zauberflöte* or *Le Nozze di Figaro* would come out on top.

_____ 2) First performed in Vienna in 1782, *Die Entführung aus dem Serail* didn't become a big success.

_____ 3) Mozart suffered headaches as he wrote it: desperate for money, he needed to write something with immediate popular appeal.

_____ 4) The story may be complicated, and there are resonances which audiences today may find discomfiting.

_____ 5) Selim decides that he does not wish to follow in the moral footsteps of someone he so despises and, with airy contempt, he lets the Christians go free.

Complete the sentences with the information from the passage.

1) It has all the _____ charm and beauty of youth—charged with a romantic vitality.

2) Yet the _____ that it is prolix has some substance: the score is one of great intricacy and brilliance, and there are moments when it seems to get carried away with itself.

3) He also _____ to write something freshly original too.

4) He decides that he does not wish to follow in the _____ of someone he so despises and, with airy contempt, he lets the Christians go free.

5) The themes would have been _____ to 18th-century audiences.

Put the following sentences in the right order according to the passage.

A. The story may be simple, but there are resonances which audiences today may find discomfiting. Konstanze, a German lady, has been seized off a boat and imprisoned in the palace of the Turkish Pasha Selim, who first tries to seduce her and then threatens torture if she does not join his harem.

B. The libretto he inherited had to be both cut and expanded, and a combination of obstinacy and inexperience—youth again!—meant that the structure and balance remain skewed.

C. But the choruses, duets and ensembles are marvels.

D. Mozart suffered headaches as he wrote it: desperate for money, he needed to write something with immediate popular appeal, but he also yearned to write something freshly original too.

E. First performed in Vienna in 1782, it quickly became a big success despite the celebrated (perhaps mythical) verdict of the Emperor Joseph II—"Too many notes, my dear Mozart!"

F. The themes would have been familiar to 18th-century audiences.

G. The difficulty of finding singers who can surmount these challenges means that *Entführung* is relatively seldom performed.

(   )——(   )——(   )——(   )——(   )——(   )——(   )

Language in Use

Fill in the blanks with the words from the word bank. Make changes when necessary.

straightforward	expand	memory	foil	laugh
commonplace	decade	dimension	flop	exception

1) The libretto he inherited had to be both cut and _____.

2) But their attempts to escape Selim's clutches are _____ and the four Europeans are told to expect execution.

3) On the other hand, Montesquieu and Voltaire had made it a _____ that Muslims could teach Christians a thing or two.

4) But without any music to animate him, he seems two-_____.

5) Because they lie high in the tenorial range and demand _____ breath and pitch control, they are also difficult to sing.

6) You can't take it too seriously, but you can't play it for _____ either.

7) A relatively _____ staging by Giorgio Strehler at the Salzburg Festival in the seventies was much admired in its day.

8) But Welsh National Opera, Scottish Opera and Opera North all _____ with their recent efforts.

9) Glyndebourne has staged four productions since the war (the most visually _____ of them designed by Oliver Messel).

10) But it's now nearly two _____ since the opera was performed here.

Translate the following paragraphs into Chinese.

I don't think it's the supreme masterpiece, but it has all the irresistible charm and beauty of youth—charged with a romantic vitality that must reflect some of the 25-year-old composer's own optimism, newly liberated from the court of the Archbishop of Salzburg.

First performed in Vienna in 1782, it quickly became a big success despite the celebrated (perhaps mythical) verdict of the Emperor Joseph II—"Too many notes, my dear Mozart!" Yet the implication that it is prolix has some substance: the score is one of great intricacy and brilliance, and there are moments when it seems to get carried away with itself.

Oral Practice

Read the passage again and discuss with your partner about Mozart's creation of the opera *The Abduction from the Seraglio*. You may use the following expressions in your discussion.

choruses	Vienna	structure and balance	beauty of youth
story	themes	moods and techniques	singers

Passage Two   A Short History of Opera

① What is it about the **fusion** of music, drama, visual arts, and dance that appeals to millions of people?

fusion *n.* 融合

② Opera, Italian for "work", is over 400 years old. History, mythology, fairy tales, folk stories, literature, and drama have inspired composers for centuries. Opera reaches beyond geographical and cultural boundaries as the most creative of all the performing arts. Where did it all begin?

③ During the Renaissance, in Florence, Italy, a small group of wealthy artists, statesmen, writers, and musicians, called the Florentine Camerata, gathered to discuss how to **revive** and transform Greek drama. They favored heightening the text by creating the solo melody or monody which would enhance natural speech. Jacopo Peri (1561–1633), composed the first acknowledged opera, *Dafne*, in the late 1590s. Claudio Monteverdi (1567–1643) is well known for his operas *Orfeo* (1607), *Arianna* (1608), *L'incoronazione di Poppea* (1642), and *Il Ritorno d'Ulisse* (1641). The latter two operas **premiered** in Venice, where the first opera house was built in 1637. By the mid-1600s, opera had spread to all of Italy and into France and Germany.

revive *v.* 使复兴

premiere *v.*（戏剧、电影等）首次公演

④　The **Baroque** period, ca. 1650–1750, brought the works of J. S. Bach (1685–1750), George Friedrich Handel (1685–1759) and Antonio Vivaldi (1678–1741) into circulation. Baroque opera flourished in the royal courts and opera houses in Europe with the Italian school at the **fore**. Handel's operas dominated the landscape in England; his operas *Rinaldo* (1710), *Giulio Cesare* (1725), and *Semele* (1744) have enjoyed a recent rebirth on today's opera stages.

Baroque *adj.* & *n.* 巴洛克（的）

fore *n.* 前部

⑤　From ca. 1750–1827, Christoph Willibald Gluck (1714–1787), Franz Joseph Haydn (1732–1809), Wolfgang Amadeus Mozart (1756–1791), and Ludwig van Beethoven (1770–1827) emerged as significant opera composers. Opera developed by expanding in structure, harmony, and plot content. The orchestra played a more important role in providing harmonic depth and variety to **accompaniments**. Structure became more flexible, i.e., the form of recitative/aria or recitative/duet expanded to include chorus, **solo ensembles**, and descriptive instrumental passages. Haydn composed over 75 operas as entertainment for the Esterhazy court; Gluck, who returned to a simpler, leaner style whose plots reverted to mythological subjects, is best remembered for his timeless *Orfeo ed Euridice* (1762); and Mozart, a supreme musical dramatist, composed operas in a variety of styles and languages. Mozart used music to specifically define his characters and plots, choosing specific keys, composing individual vocal lines in solo ensembles, and creating ingenious **orchestrations** to "paint" emotions. Mozart brilliantly composed in several different operatic forms: **opera seria** (*Idomeneo* 1781), Singspiel (*Abduction from the Seraglio* 1782), and **dramma giocoso** (*Don Giovanni* 1787).

accompaniment *n.* 伴奏

solo ensemble 合奏

orchestration *n.* 管弦乐编曲

opera seria 悲歌剧；正歌剧

dramma giocoso 诙谐戏剧

⑥　During the 1820s, after the French Revolution, a new middle class began to frequent the theaters in search of entertainment. Composers turned to the literature of Shakespeare, Hugo, Goethe rather than to Greek mythology, efforting to present operas that these audiences would appreciate. Grand opera incorporated all artistic elements: beautiful solo voices, chorus, ballet, elaborate scenery-spectacle, in short. Lighter opera fare, including Opéra

Comique (Jacques Offenbach's *La Périchole* 1868) less pretentious and often more comic than Grand Opera and **Operetta** also emerged during this period. Opera **buffa** in Italy (Gaetano Donizetti's *Don Pasquale* 1843), operetta in Austria (Johann Strauss, Jr.'s *Die Fledermaus* 1874), and operetta in England (Gilbert and Sullivan's *H.M.S. Pinafore* 1878), developed loyal followings. Bridging the Classical and Romantic periods, Georges Bizet's (1838–1875) *Carmen* (1875) provided exotic locations, romantic, evocative, and memorable musical themes, and high drama.

operetta *n.* 轻歌剧；小歌剧

buffa *n.* 唱谐角的女歌剧演唱家

❼ From ca. 1817–1900, Romanticism and Impressionism took the art world by storm. Italy's native composers Gioachino Rossini (1792–1868), Vincenzo Bellini (1801–1835) and Gaetano Donizetti (1797–1848) composed operas in the opera buffa and opera lirica styles. These three composers inspired their singers to sing in the bel canto style, executing long, elegantly and beautifully phrased, often challenging, vocal lines. Their operas are vehicles for the expert singer. Rossini's *La Cenerentola* [*Cinderella*] (1817) requires **fioritura** technique and comic timing from its entire cast; Bellini's *Norma* (1831) demands a coloratura soprano with superb dramatic skills; Donizetti's *La fille du Régiment* (1840) requires both a brilliant coloratura soprano and a tenor with limitless high C's. Witty sung dialogue, sharply etched characters, and beautifully crafted vocal lines ensure the success of these operas. On the heels of these composers came Giuseppe Verdi (1813–1901) whose many operas remain the **backbone** of current opera house **repertoire**. In Italy, Verdi is lauded as a patriot, statesman, and the composer of politically controversial topics of his day. His operas are memorable because of the dramatically beautiful, challenging, and memorable vocal melodies he crafted for all of his characters. With the exception of Verdi's last opera, the comic *Falstaff* (1893), his operas are based on dramatic plays and texts, among which are Shakespeare's *Macbeth* (1847), *Othello* (1887), *Falstaff* (1893), Victor Hugo's *Rigoletto* (1851), Alexandre Dumas' *La Traviata* (1853), along with some of his politically based librettos: *Nabucco* (1842), *I due Foscari* (1844) and *Aida* (1871).

fioritura *n.* [意大利语]【音乐】花（腔）音（歌曲中的装饰音）

backbone *n.* 支柱

repertoire *n.* 全部节目

8 The symbiotic relationship between literature and music strengthened as the 19th century unfolded. Richard Wagner (1813–1883) created a new genre of opera whereby the function of music was to serve dramatic expression. *The Ring Cycle* used Norse mythology and **leitmotifs** to cohesively bind four operas together using musical themes for characters, situations, and ideas. Wagner composed for massive orchestrations, increasing the orchestra size from 5060 to 90100 players. Richard Strauss (1864–1949) followed in Wagner's footsteps using even more **lush** orchestrations, introducing dissonance (clashing tonal centers) as an expressive and descriptive tool to underline the drama. Among his most well-known operas are *Salomé* (1905), *Elektra* (1909), *Der Rosenkavalier* (1911) and *Ariadne auf Naxos* (1912).

leitmotif *n.* 主乐调，乐旨

lush *adj.* 豪华的

9 Toward the end of the Romantic period, Claude Debussy (1862–1918) and Maurice Ravel (1875–1937) explored musical Impressionism by stretching **tonality** and form. Debussy's one successful opera, *Pelléas et Mélisande* (1902), is based on the symbolist play by Maurice Maeterlinck, and Ravel's delightful opera *L'enfant et les Sortilèges* [*The Child and the Spells*] (1925) places singers in the orchestra pit to vocally depict the items in the child's room as they come to life on stage. Meanwhile, in Italy, Giacomo Puccini (1858–1924) had taken up Verdi's challenge. Puccini composed in the "verismo" [truth] style, choosing to present everyday people caught in extraordinarily challenging and melodramatic circumstances. Puccini's operas are musically visceral and emotionally bold. He composed for larger voices using rich, full orchestrations. Some of his most well-known operas are *Manon Lescaut* (1893), *La Bohème* (1896), *Tosca* (1900), *Madama Butterfly* (1904), and *La Fanciulla del West [The Girl of the Golden West]* (1910). Other Italian verismo composers are Francesco Cilea (1866–1950) who composed *Adriana Lecouvreur* in 1902, Umberto Giordano (1867–1948) known for his opera *Andrea Chénier* (1896), Ruggero Leoncavallo (1857–1919) remembered for I *Pagliacci* (1892), and Pietro Mascagni (1863–1945) who composed *Cavalleria Rusticanain* (1890). The latter two operas are frequently performed **on a double bill**. All verismo operas require

tonality *n.* 音调

on a double bill 一起（演出）

mature voices and dramatic singers who are convincing on stage.

10 As drama became more important to the portrayals of characters on stage, composers of the 20th century began to create operas for the actor/singer. Kurt Weill (1900–1950), known for *Lost Under the Stars* (1949), Igor Stravinsky (1882–1971), who composed *The Rake's Progress* in 1951, and Benjamin Britten (1913–1976) remembered for *Peter Grimes* (1945) and *Albert Herring* (1947) among many others, all composed in a less tonal idiom with more focus on the drama of the story. The operatic singers who tackle these roles need to be excellent musicians, vocal technicians and superb actors. Opera composers of the 20th century experimented with **polytonality** (more than one key occurring simultaneously), minimalism (music with repetitive structures), and **theatricality**. Austrians Arnold Schönberg (1874–1951), who composed the **monologue** opera, *Erwartung [Expectation]* in 1924, and his pupil, Alban Berg (1885–1935), who composed the chiller, *Wozzeck*, in 1925, turned to psychological dramas. In contrast, American composers George Gershwin (1898–1937), beloved for his *Porgy and Bess* (1935), Carlisle Floyd (b. 1926) who set the Tennessee story, *Susanna* in 1955, and Aaron Copland (1900–1990) whose midwestern setting of *The Tender Land* (1954) was originally conceived for television, composed operas on historical and social Americana themes. In further contrast, Philip Glass's (b. 1937) *Einstein on the Beach* (1976) and *Akhnaten* (1984), and John Adams's (b. 1947) *Nixon in China* (1987) and *The Death of Klinghoffer* (1991) explore minimalism more in depth while John Corigliano's (b. 1938) *The Ghosts of Versailles* (1991), commissioned by the Metropolitan Opera, Mark Adamo's (b. 1962) *Little Women* (1998), and William Bolcom's (b. 1938) *A View from the Bridge* (1999), continue to explore ensemble operas, where the focus is on the ensemble rather than the solo singer.

polytonality *n.* 多调性

theatricality *n.* 戏剧风格；夸张

monologue *n.* 独白

11 In the 21st century, opera composers to note are: Jake Heggie (b. 1961) for *Dead Man Walking* (2000), John Adams (1947) for *Doctor Atomic* (2005), Osvaldo Golijov (b. 1960) for *Ainadamar* (2005), and Tan Dun (b. 1956) for *The First Emperor* (2006). All

these operas have enjoyed recent successful productions in major
U.S. opera houses.

 Extended Activities

Each of the following statements contains information given in one of
the paragraphs in the passage. Identify the paragraph from which the
information is derived and put the corresponding number in the space
provided.

_____ 1) Opera has some universal values which go beyond cultures and is regarded
as the most creative of all the performing arts.

_____ 2) These three composers inspired their singers to sing in the bel canto style,
which is beautiful and elegant but challenging.

_____ 3) By the mid-1600s, opera had been accepted everywhere in Italy and into
some other European countries.

_____ 4) Music is what Mozart used to shape characters and tell stories. He chose
specific keys, composed individual vocal lines in solo ensembles, and created
ingenious orchestrations to "paint" emotions.

_____ 5) Baroque operas were enjoyed both by the royalty as well as by common people
in Europe with the Italian school at the fore.

_____ 6) Opera developed by expanding in structure, harmony, and story-telling.

_____ 7) Composers turned to the literature of Shakespeare, Hugo, and Goethe rather
than to Greek mythology in order to win the audience's love.

_____ 8) The literature and music developed a stronger and closer relationship as the
19th century unfolded.

_____ 9) As characters' importance was promoted in operas, composers of the 20th
century began to create operas for the actor/singer.

_____ 10) In Italy, Verdi is lauded as a patriot, statesman, and the composer of works on
political issues of his day.

Answer the following questions based on the understanding of the passage.

1) When and where did the history of opera begin?

2) Whose works were in circulation in the Baroque period?

3) What were the changes to opera styles from ca. 1750–1827?

4) Who did composers turn to during the 1820s?

5) What did composers do to opera styles toward the end of the Romantic period?

Translate the following paragraph into English.

19 世纪 20 年代，法国大革命之后，新兴中产阶级开始频繁出现在剧院中以寻求消遣。作曲家们开始将目光转向莎士比亚、雨果和歌德的文学，而非借鉴希腊神话，以此迎合新的观众群体。大型歌剧融合了所有艺术元素，简单地说，包括了优美的独唱、合唱、芭蕾以及精致的场景布置。各种轻松的歌剧形式，包括比大歌剧更自然且更富喜剧色彩的喜歌剧（如雅克·奥芬巴赫的《拉·佩利肖尔》）以及轻歌剧都诞生于这一时期。

 # Exploring

Work in groups to make a presentation on the history of operas. Your group work can be divided into the following steps.

Step 1   Search online for relevant information based on the clues in the passage.

Step 2   Work out the timeline of opera history including representatives, works, styles, etc.

Step 3   Put the information on your slides and make a presentation in front of the whole class.

 # Mini-pedia

Sydney Opera House

Inaugurated in 1973, the Sydney Opera House is a great architectural work of the 20th century that brings together multiple strands of creativity and innovation in both architectural form and structural design. A great urban sculpture set in a remarkable waterscape, at the tip of a peninsula projecting into Sydney Harbour, the building has had an enduring influence on architecture. The Sydney Opera House comprises three groups of interlocking vaulted "shells" which roof two main performance halls and a restaurant. These shell-structures are set upon a vast platform and are surrounded by terrace areas that function as pedestrian concourses. In 1957, when the project of the Sydney Opera House was awarded by an international jury to Danish architect Jørn Utzon, it marked a radically new approach to construction.

The Sydney Opera House constitutes a masterpiece of 20th-century architecture. Its significance is based on its unparalleled design and construction; its exceptional engineering achievements and technological innovation and its position as a world-famous icon of architecture. It is a daring and visionary experiment that has had an enduring influence on the emergent architecture of the late 20th century. Utzon's original design concept and his unique approach to building gave impetus to a collective creativity of architects, engineers and builders. Ove Arup's engineering achievements helped make Utzon's vision a reality. The design represents an extraordinary interpretation and response to the setting in Sydney Harbour. The Sydney Opera House is also of outstanding universal value for its achievements in structural engineering and building technology. The building is a great artistic monument and an icon, accessible to society at large.

All elements necessary to express the values of the Sydney Opera House are included within the boundaries of the nominated area and buffer zone. This ensures the complete representation of its significance as an architectural object of great beauty in its waterscape setting. The Sydney Opera House continues to perform its function as a world-class performing arts centre. The Conservation Plan specifies the need to balance the roles of the building as an architectural monument and as a state of the art performing centre, thus retaining its authenticity of use and function. Attention given to retaining the building's authenticity culminated with the Conservation Plan and the Utzon Design Principles.

The Sydney Opera House was included in the National Heritage List in 2005 under the Environment Protection and Biodiversity Conservation Act 1999 and on the State

Heritage Register of New South Wales in 2003 under the Heritage Act 1977. Listing in the National Heritage List implies that any proposed action to be taken inside or outside the boundaries of a National Heritage place or a World Heritage property that may have a significant impact on the heritage values is prohibited without the approval of the Minister for the Environment and Heritage. A buffer zone has been established.

The present state of conservation is very good. The property is maintained and preserved through regular and rigorous repair and conservation programmes. The management system of the Sydney Opera House takes into account a wide range of measures provided under planning and heritage legislation and policies of both the Australian Government and the New South Wales Government. The Management Plan for the Sydney Opera House, the Conservation Plan and the Utzon Design Principles together provide the policy framework for the conservation and management of the Sydney Opera House.

 # Reflection

Achievements	Yes	No
I am familiar with the general stages of opera's development in history and its representatives.		
I have understood the changes in opera styles throughout history.		
I have acquired some words and expressions related to opera.		

MEDIA

INTERNET

TELEVISION

RADIO

NEWSPA

ZINES

UNIT 13

MEDIA

◇

GOALS

1 To familiarize with the nature and performance of media violence;

2 To become aware of the negative effects of media;

3 To understand some issues about digital literacy;

4 To acquire useful words and expressions related to the topic of media.

Warming-up

Answer the following questions:

1. What do you know about media?
2. What is "media violence"? Can you name some examples of "media violence"?
3. What can we do to reduce media violence?

Reading

Passage One Media Violence and the Resulting Effect on Children

❶　Violence is an extreme form of aggression, such as **assault**, rape or murder. Violence has many causes, including frustration and exposure to violent media. Exposure to violence in media, including television, movies, music, and video games, represents a significant risk to the health of children and adolescents. It is an increasing problem in modern society. The scope and efficiency of violent behavior has had serious consequences. A large proportion of children's media exposure includes acts of violence that are witnessed or "virtually **perpetrated**" (in the form of video games) by young people. Media violence plays an important role in the analysis of violent behavior. While it is difficult to determine which children who have experienced televised violence are at greatest risk, there appears to be a strong relation between media violence and aggressive behavior.

assault *n.* 袭击

perpetrate *v.* 犯罪；作恶

②   Televised violence results in aggressive behavior. It has demonstrated that very young children will imitate aggressive acts on TV in their play with peers. Children are unable to distinguish between fact and fantasy and may view violence as an ordinary occurrence. In general, violence on television and in movies often conveys a model of conflict resolution. It is efficient, frequent, and significant. Heroes are violent, and, as such, are rewarded for their behavior. They become role models for youth. Television, movies, and music videos normalize carrying and using weapons and **glamorize** them as a source of personal power. Children are influenced by media; they learn by observing, imitating, and adopting behaviors. Interactive media, such as video games and the Internet, are relatively new media forms with even greater potential for positive and negative effects on children's physical and mental health. Exposure online to violent scenes has been associated with increased aggressive behavior. In many games, the child or teenager is "embedded" in the game and uses a "joystick" (handheld controller) that enhances both the experience and the aggressive feelings. These activities make them insensitive towards their surrounding people. It should be stopped before it becomes a more serious issue for our society.

glamorize v. 渲染

③   Psychology professor Dave Grossman (2000) indicates that there are four primary military training techniques that violent media indirectly utilizes to impact children: brutalization, classical conditioning, operant conditioning and role modelling. Brutalization is centered around the concept of losing all **remnants** of individuality and accepting violence and discipline as a new and necessary worldly skill (Grossman, 2000).

remnant n. 残余

④   Secondly, Grossman identifies classical conditioning as a technique used to influence children to make associations. He describes it as a "conditioning in which the conditioned stimulus (the sound of a bell) is paired with and precedes the unconditioned stimulus (the sight of food) until the conditioned stimulus alone is sufficient to elicit the response (salivation in a dog)". Grossman (2000) explains as such: This technique is so morally

reprehensible that there are very few examples of it in modern U.S. military training, but the media is doing it to our children. Kids watch vivid images of human death and suffering, and they learn to associate it with: laughter, cheers, popcorn, soda, and their girlfriend's perfume (classical conditioning).

reprehensible *adj.* 应受谴责的

⑤ Similar to classical conditioning, Grossman next speaks of operant conditioning. It is "conditioning in which the desired behavior or increasingly closer **approximations** to it are followed by a rewarding or reinforcing stimulus" (Operant Conditioning). Violent video games directly parallel this psychological principle. Clearly, this violent and interactive form of media **subtly** prompts children's psyche to adopt the ability and will to kill.

approximation *n.* 近似值

subtly *adv.* 隐隐约约地

⑥ Lastly, the technique of using role models to set an archetype, is often used by the media. This method is quite self-explanatory in the sense that the media glorifies violent heroes and **instills** in children the notion that violence is the greatest problem-solving skill.

instill *v.* 灌输

⑦ Evidence of this theory is prevalent in modern day society. Most recently, the Sandy Hook elementary school shootings of 2013 where 20 children and 6 adults were brutally gunned down by Adam Lanza, were very similar to the Paducah school shootings. There have been many such **copycat** killer scenarios. Therefore, the use of these military theories and techniques in the creation of violent media, directly correlate between media violence and homicide among children.

copycat *n.* 模仿者

⑧ Grossman (2000) concludes that: we need to work toward "legislation" which **outlaws** violent video games for children. In July 2000, the city of Indianapolis passed just such an **ordinance**, and every other city, country or state in America has the right to do the same. There is no Constitutional "right" to teach children to blow people's heads off at the local video **arcade**. And we are very close to being able to do to the media, through "**litigation**," which

outlaw *v.* 宣传不合法
ordinance *n.* 案例；法规

arcade *n.* 游戏厅
litigation *n.* 诉讼

is being done to the tobacco industry, hurting them in the only place they understand their wallets.

Reading Comprehension

Decide whether the following statements are true or false. Write T for true and F for false.

_____ 1) The children who have experienced televised violence tend to be more aggressive than those who haven't.

_____ 2) Violence on television and in movies often conveys a model of conflict resolution.

_____ 3) Video games and the Internet are relatively new media forms with even greater potential for only negative effects on children's physical and mental health.

_____ 4) Operant conditioning is used to influence children to make associations.

_____ 5) We should do something to reduce the negative effects of media, through "litigation," which is being done to the tobacco industry.

Complete the sentences with the information from the passage.

1) Violence has many causes, including frustration, and _____ to violent media.

2) Heroes are violent, and, as such, are _____ for their behavior. They become role models for youth.

3) There are four primary military training techniques that violent media indirectly utilizes to impact children: _____, _____, _____, and _____.

4) Operant conditioning is a conditioning in which the desired behavior or increasingly closer approximations to it are followed by _____.

5) We need to work toward "_____" which outlaws violent video games for children.

Put the following sentences in the right order according to the sequence the author presents the media effects on children.

A. Kids watch vivid images of human death and suffering and they learn to associate it with: laughter, cheers, popcorn, soda, and their girlfriend's perfume.

B. There appears to be a strong relation between media violence and aggressive behavior.

C. Role models is a self-explanatory method in the sense that the media glorifies violent heroes.

D. In many games, the child or teenager is "embedded" in the game and uses a "joystick" that enhances both the experience and the aggressive feelings.

E. Brutalization is centered around the concept of losing all remnants of individuality and accepting violence and discipline as a new and necessary worldly skill.

F. Operant Conditioning subtly prompts children's psyche to adopt the ability and will to kill.

(   )——(   )——(   )——(   )——(   )——(   )

Language in Use

Fill in the blanks with the words or phrases from the word bank. Make changes when necessary.

assault	reward	exposure	demonstrate	distinguish
convey	outlaw	similar to	prevalent	subtly

1) Fares do not include _____ between railway stations and steamer piers.

2) We were given a brief _____ of the machine's functions.

3) The male bird is _____ from the female by its red beak.

4) A(n) _____ on the capital was launched in the early hours of the morning and luckily there was no report for the casualties recently.

5) A bonus of up to 5 per cent can be added to a pupil's final exam marks as a _____ for good spelling, punctuation and grammar.

6) His stance towards the story is quite _____ ours, so it is not difficult to follow him at the very beginning of reading.

7) The novelist _____ brings to life the inner world of his character.

8) The legislation would _____ discrimination in employment, housing and education.

9) Those immigrant teenagers who easily rebel against traditional Chinese culture are _____ to western values in their early childhood.

10) Justice will _____ over brutality.

Translate the following paragraph into Chinese.

Violence is an extreme form of aggression, such as assault, rape or murder. Violence has many causes, including frustration and exposure to violent media. Exposure to violence in media, including television, movies, music, and video games, represents a significant risk to the health of children and adolescents. It is an increasing problem in modern society. The scope and efficiency of violent behavior has had serious consequences. A large proportion of children's media exposure includes acts of violence that are witnessed or "virtually perpetrated" (in the form of video games) by young people.

 Oral Practice

 Read the passage again and discuss with your partner about media violence. You may use the following expressions in your discussion.

media violence exposure	witness	television	aggressive
classical conditioning	heroes	rewarded	video games
operant conditioning	stimulus	reinforce	

Passage Two How Literacy Is Changing

By Ernest Morrell

❶   We are living during a time of communications revolution. In just a short span, the mechanisms by which we access and produce information have been completely transformed, changing the fabric of our very lives and producing a generation unlike any we've ever seen. The first time I heard about the "Internet" in 1993 I could literally speak to one another and share information via telephone lines! It seemed more like science fiction than *Star Trek*, but I watched in awe as the technology support director of the Graduate School of Education at the University of California at Berkeley "surfed" the World Wide Web and visited libraries and universities from his personal computer.

❷   Later that year I dialed up the Internet at my parents' home while my teenage brothers looked over my shoulder in anticipation. A sign popped up on the screen congratulating us, but we couldn't find the Web. Instead there was a blank screen with a blinking **cursor** waiting for me to type something. After some research my brother **surmised** that we needed a URL (uniform resource locator, more commonly known now as a Web address), so he found a few and we were off. Within a week we had figured out the logic of the ".com" Web address, we had gotten software for a "Web-browser," and we were hooked, even if it took an entire evening to visit three sites, and no one could reach my parents for hours because we were dominating the main telephone line.

cursor n. 光标

surmise v. 推测；猜想

3 That was in 1993. Nearly 20 years later, our world is no longer the same. I type this article on a laptop computer from my bed while uploading files into my Dropbox, a file-hosting service that offers cloud storage and file **synchronization**. With cloud computing, I can access my files from my laptop, my desktop at work, my tablet, or my mobile device. I can also access my electronic mail and visit Internet sites through my Google search engine to make certain that my use of computer **terminology** is accurate.

synchronization n. 同步

terminology n. 术语

4 To my left is my Android smartphone (I call it a mobile, because it is much more than a phone) that keeps time via satellite and allows me to listen to music, text messages to my friends and family (even my mom text messages me), capture digital photographs and small amounts of digital film, play video games, check the Internet, and talk on the phone while trying to finish this "article" under deadline! I place *article* in quotes because what I really have is one long text file that I edit via Google Docs, and there is a chance that you will be reading this from an iPad, a Nook or Kindle, or some other electronic device that is devoid of paper and ink. There are no wires connecting me to anything.

5 Now, welcome to the second decade of the 21st century, where information has been globalized, digitized, and sped up to move at the speed of thought. Being **literate** in this new world means understanding everything I just wrote, as well as knowing about mp3s and jpegs and.wav files. It means being able to

literate adj. 有识读能力的

program HTML on your personal websites (or blogs, or wikis) and sending e-mails from your mobile or tablet in a taxicab or uploading pictures from your phone into your Picasa library on your laptop. It also means being endlessly connected to "friends" via Facebook, Twitter, or any other number of social media sites whose users now numbers in the hundreds of millions!

6 In the world of business, it means communicating with colleagues all over the world simultaneously with the press of a button from under your covers before you've had your morning coffee. In the world of personal communication, it means carrying a computer, a **rolodex**, and a calendar in your **hip** pocket and never losing touch. And our students are products of this world. They, for the most part, have unusual command of some of these technologies. Some have called these youth "digital natives." I prefer to think of them as products of our times.

rolodex *n.* 名片盒
hip *n.* 臀部

7 However, for all of their digital expertise, there is still a great deal that these youth have to learn about how to process the information that they are **inundated** with via these new portals of information. They also need to develop the skills to be able to create information that can be shared via websites, digital photographs and film, and online journal spaces like weblogs. All of these methods of accessing, processing, and **disseminating** information can be loosely associated under the umbrella of 21st-century literacies.

inundate *v.* 淹没；使充满

disseminate *v.* 散布，传播

Extended Activities

1 Each of the following statements contains information given in one of the paragraphs in the passage. Identify the paragraph from which the information is derived and put the corresponding number in the space provided.

_____ 1) With cloud computing, I can access my files from my laptop, my desktop at work, my tablet, or my mobile device.

_____ 2) Director of the Graduate School of Education at the University of California at Berkeley "surfed" the World Wide Web and visited libraries and universities from his personal computer.

_____ 3) I can endlessly connect to "friends" via Facebook, Twitter, or any other number of social media sites.

_____ 4) It took us an entire evening to visit three sites, and no one could reach my parents for hours because we were dominating the main telephone line.

_____ 5) With my Android smartphone, I can keep time via satellite, listen to music, text messages to my friends and family, and capture digital photographs.

_____ 6) The youth are known as the "digital natives".

_____ 7) The youth also need to develop the skills to be able to create information that can be shared via websites, digital photographs and film, and online journal spaces like weblogs.

Write a summary of the article by using the clues given below.

communication revolution	"Internet" in 1993	access
"digital natives"	create information	digital
Facebook and Twitter	telephone line	literate
cloud computing	web browser	surf
personal computer	Google search	URL
web address	smartphone	laptop

Translate the following paragraph into English.

一般情况下，我们会将笔记本电脑和台式电脑用于商务和一般家庭用途，并使用计算机网络来进行通信、文字处理、跟踪金融行市以及玩游戏。这些电脑拥有大量内存以存储成百上千的程序和文件。它们配备有键盘、鼠标、光标球或者其他的设备，还会有一个视频显示器或液晶显示器来显示信息。

Exploring

Work in groups to discuss the topic of media violence. Your group work can be divided into the following steps.

Step 1 Search for information about the topic of media violence, such as its categories, causes and solutions.

Step 2 Work in groups to collect all the information and make some notes.

Step 3 Give a group presentation in class.

Mini-pedia

Media Violence in America

The World Health Organization has defined violence as "the intentional use of physical force or power, threatened or actual, against oneself, another person, or against a group or community, which either results in or has a high likelihood of resulting in injury, death, psychological harm, mal-development, or deprivation."

Violence occurs at an alarming rate in the United States. Among Americans aged 15 to 34 years, two of the top three causes of death are homicide and suicide. In a given year, more U.S. children will die from gunfire than will die from cancer, pneumonia, influenza, asthma, and HIV/AIDS combined.

The rate of firearm-related death or injury in the United States is the highest among industrialized countries, with more than 32,000 deaths each year. In recent years, this has meant that 88 people die each day from firearm-related homicides, suicides, and unintentional deaths. Further, the number of nonfatal injuries due to firearms is more than double the number of deaths.

While there are multiple factors that lead to violent actions, a growing body of literature shows a strong association between the perpetration of violence and the exposure to violence through the media.

Reflection

Achievements	Yes	No
I am familiar with the nature and performance of media violence.		
I am aware of the negative effects of media.		
I have understood some issues about digital literacy.		
I have acquired useful words and expressions related to the topic of media.		

UNIT 14

PRESIDENTIAL ELECTION

GOALS

1 To understand the function of campaign finance in the presidential election of the U.S.;

2 To familiarize with the language style of a presidential inauguration speech;

3 To become aware of the differences in political culture between China and the U.S.;

4 To acquire some words and expressions related to presidential election.

Warming-up

Answer the following questions:

1. Is money important in the presidential election of the U.S.?
2. Where does financing of the presidential election come from?
3. In what tone should a presidential inaugural address be, in your opinion?

Reading

Passage One Campaign Finance

❶ The United States is a federal republic, with elected officials at the federal (national), state and local levels. On a national level, the head of state, the President, is elected indirectly by the people of each state, through an Electoral College. The funding of electoral campaigns has always been a **controversial** issue in American politics. **Infringement** of free speech (First Amendment) is an argument against restrictions on campaign contributions, while **allegations** of corruption arising from unlimited contributions and the need for political equality are arguments for the other side. Private funds are a major source of finance in the electoral campaign, from individuals and organizations. The first attempt to regulate campaign finance by **legislation** was in 1867, but major legislation, with the intention to widely enforce, on campaign finance was not introduced until the 1970s.

controversial *adj.* 有争议的
infringement *n.* 侵犯

allegation *n.* 断言；主张

legislation *n.* 立法

❷ Money contributed to campaigns can be classified into two parts: "hard money" and "soft money". Hard money is money contributed directly to a campaign, by an individual or organization. Soft money is money from an individual or organization not contributed to a campaign, but spent in candidate specific advertising or other efforts that benefits that candidate by groups supporting the candidate, but legally not coordinated by the official campaign.

❸   The **Federal Election Campaign Act** of 1971 required candidates to **disclose** sources of campaign contributions and campaign **expenditure**. It was **amended** in 1974 to legally limit campaign contributions. It **banned** direct contributing to campaigns by corporations and trade unions and limited individual donations to $1,000 per campaign. It introduced public funding for Presidential primaries and elections. The Act also placed limits of $5,000 per campaign on **PACs** (political action committees). The limits on individual contributions and prohibition of direct corporate or labor union campaigns led to a huge increase in the number of PACs. Today many labor unions and corporations have their own PACs, and over 4,000 in total exist. The 1974 amendment also specified a Federal Election Commission, created in 1975 to administer and enforce campaign finance law. Various other **provisions** were also included, such as a ban on contributions or expenditures by foreign nationals (incorporated from the Foreign Agents Registration Act (FARA) (1966)).

❹   The case of Buckley v. Valeo (1976) challenged the Act. Most provisions were upheld, but the court found that the **mandatory** spending limit imposed was unconstitutional, as was the limit placed on campaign spending from the candidate's personal fortune and the provision that limited independent expenditures by individuals and organizations supporting but not officially linked to a campaign. The effect of the first decision was to allow candidates such as Ross Perot and Steve Forbes to spend enormous amounts of their own money in their own campaigns. The effect of the second decision was to allow the culture of "soft money" to develop.

Federal Election Campaign
Act 联邦选举法

disclose *v.* 透露，公开

expenditure *n.* 支出，花费

amend *v.* 修正

ban *v.* 禁止

PAC 政治行动委员会

provision *n.* 条款，规定

mandatory *adj.* 强制的，必须的

⑤ A 1979 amendment to the Federal Election Campaign Act allowed political parties to spend without limit on get-out-the-vote and voter registration activities conducted primarily for a presidential candidate. Later, they were permitted by FECA to use "soft money", unregulated, unlimited contributions to fund this effort. Increasingly, the money began to be spent on issue advertising, candidate specific advertising that was being funded mostly by soft money.

⑥ The **Bipartisan Campaign Reform Act** of 2002 banned local and national parties from spending "soft money" and banned national party committees from accepting or spending soft money. It increased the limit of contributions by individuals from $1,000 to $2,000. It banned corporations or labor unions from funding issue advertising directly, and banned the use of corporate or labor money for advertisements that mention a federal candidate within 60 days of a general election or 30 days of a primary. The constitutionality of the bill was challenged and in December 2003, the Supreme Court upheld most provisions of the legislation.

Bipartisan Campaign Reform Act 两党竞选改革法

⑦ A large number of "527 groups" were active for the first time in the 2004 election. These groups receive donations from individuals and groups and then spend the money on issue **advocacy**, such as the anti-Kerry ads by Swift Boat Veterans For Truth. This is a new form of soft money, and not surprisingly it is controversial. Many 527 groups have close links with the Democratic or Republican Parties, even though legally they cannot coordinate their activities with them. John McCain, one of the Senators behind the Bipartisan Campaign Reform Act, and President Bush have both declared a desire to ban 527s.

advocacy n. 拥护，提倡

⑧ Changing campaign finance laws is a highly controversial issue. Some reformers wish to see laws changed in order to improve electoral competition and political equality. Opponents wish to see the system stay as it is, whereas other reformers wish even fewer restrictions on the freedom to spend and contribute money. The Supreme Court has made it increasingly difficult for those who wish to regulate election financing, but options like partial public funding of campaigns are still possible and offer the potential to address reformers' concerns with minimal restrictions on the freedom to contribute.

Reading Comprehension

1. Decide whether the following statements are true or false. Write T for true and F for false.

_____ 1) The major legislation, with the intention to widely enforce, on campaign finance was not introduced until 1867.

_____ 2) The amendment of the Federal Election Campaign Act of 1971 legally limited campaign contributions.

_____ 3) Today over 4,000 PACs in total exist belonging to labor unions and corporations.

_____ 4) In the case of Buckley v. Valeo (1976), the court found that the mandatory spending limit imposed was constitutional.

_____ 5) Many 527 groups legally coordinate their activities with the Democratic or Republican Parties.

2. Answer the following questions based on the understanding of the passage.

1) What is the difference between hard money and soft money?

2) What is included in the 1974 amendment?

3) What is the difference between the Federal Election Campaign Act of 1971 and the Bipartisan Campaign Reform Act in terms of limit to contributions by individuals?

4) What was the influence of the Buckley v. Valeo case on American campaign finance laws?

5) Why is it highly controversial to change campaign finance laws?

Language in Use

Fill in the blanks with the words from the word bank. Make changes when necessary.

| advocacy | controversial | ban | expenditure | disclose |
| allegation | infringement | amend | mandatory | provision |

1) Henry _____ the speech by making some additions of his personal experience.
2) Their _____ and action inspires us to fight to end campus violence.
3) The issue of the death penalty is highly _____ all over the world.
4) The local government has introduced _____ drug testing in high crime areas.
5) Daybreak _____ a chain of mountains in the distance.
6) What happens if we have a patent _____?
7) The dictator _____ all newspapers and books that criticized his regime.
8) The suspect then responds to each _____ by admitting, denying or objecting to it.
9) The gap between income and _____ last year has widened to 11%.
10) No one quite knows which _____ of the Constitution justified the outcome.

Rewrite each sentence with the given word and change the word form when necessary.

1) He often complained that the climate change resulted in his physical illness. (arise)

_____

2) He tried to stop the thief, only to be knocked down by a running car. (attempt)

_____

3) Adolescents are not allowed to drink and buy alcohol in this country. (prohibition)

_____

4) The local government finds it hard to carry out the law against gambling in public places. (enforce)

_____

5) Only adults are admitted membership into the club. (restriction)

_____

Translate the following paragraphs into Chinese.

1) The funding of electoral campaigns has always been a controversial issue in American politics. Infringement of free speech (First Amendment) is an argument against restrictions on campaign contributions, while allegations of corruption arising

from unlimited contributions and the need for political equality are arguments for the other side.

2) Changing campaign finance laws is a highly controversial issue. Some reformers wish to see laws changed in order to improve electoral competition and political equality. Opponents wish to see the system stay as it is, whereas other reformers wish even fewer restrictions on the freedom to spend and contribute money.

 Oral Practice

6 Work in groups to discuss the question below, and then each group is required to make a presentation by turns: As a presidential candidate of the U.S., which factor is more influential on the electoral result: wealth or aptitude?

Passage Two President Barack Obama's First Inauguration Speech

(An excerpt)

1 My fellow citizens: I stand here today humbled by the task before us, grateful for the trust you've bestowed, mindful of the sacrifices borne by our ancestors.

2 I thank President Bush for his service to our nation—as well as the generosity and cooperation he has shown throughout this transition. Forty-four Americans have now taken the presidential **oath**. The words have been spoken during rising tides of prosperity and the still waters of peace. Yet, every so often, the oath is taken amidst gathering clouds and raging storms. At these moments, America has carried on not simply because of the skill or vision of those in high office, but because we, the people, have remained faithful to the ideals of our **forebears** and true to our founding documents.

oath *n.* 誓言

forebear *n.* 祖先

3 That we are in the midst of a crisis is now well understood. Our nation is at war against a far-reaching network of violence and hatred. Our economy is badly weakened, a consequence of greed and irresponsibility on the part of some, but also our collective failure to make hard choices and prepare the nation for a new age. Homes have been lost, jobs shed, businesses **shuttered**. Our health care is too costly, our schools fail too many—and each day brings further evidence that the ways we use energy strengthen our **adversaries** and threaten our planet.

shutter *v.* 使停业

adversary *n.* 对手

④　Today I say to you that the challenges we face are real. They are serious, and they are many. They will not be met easily or in a short span of time. But know this America: They will be met.

⑤　For everywhere we look, there is work to be done. The state of our economy calls for action, bold and swift. And we will act, not only to create new jobs, but to lay a new foundation for growth. We will build the roads and bridges, the electric grids and digital lines that feed our commerce and bind us together. We'll restore science to its rightful place, and **wield** technology's wonders to raise health care's quality and lower its cost. We will **harness** the sun and the winds and the soil to fuel our cars and run our factories. And we will transform our schools and colleges and universities to meet the demands of a new age. All this we can do. All this we will do.

wield *v.* 使用，掌握
harness *v.* 利用

⑥　The question we ask today is not whether our government is too big or too small, but whether it works—whether it helps families find jobs at a decent wage, care they can afford, a retirement that is dignified. Where the answer is yes, we intend to move forward. Where the answer is no, programs will end. And those of us who manage the public's dollars will be held to account, to spend wisely, reform bad habits, and do our business in the light of day, because only then can we restore the vital trust between a people and their government.

⑦　Nor is the question before us whether the market is a force for good or ill. Its power to **generate** wealth and expand freedom is unmatched. But this crisis has reminded us that without a watchful eye, the market can spin out of control. The nation cannot

generate *v.* 产生，引起

prosper long when it favors only the prosperous. The success of our economy has always depended not just on the size of our gross domestic product, but on the reach of our prosperity, on the ability to extend opportunity to every willing heart—not out of charity, but because it is the surest route to our common good.

prosper *v.* 繁荣，昌盛

⑧ And so, to all the other peoples and governments who are watching today, from the grandest capitals to the small village where my father was born, know that America is a friend of each nation, and every man, woman and child who seeks a future of peace and dignity. And we are ready to lead once more.

⑨ Recall that earlier generations faced down fascism not just with missiles and tanks, but with the **sturdy alliances** and enduring convictions. They understood that our power alone cannot protect us, nor does it **entitle** us to do as we please. Instead they knew that our power grows through its prudent use; our security emanates from the justness of our cause, the force of our example, the tempering qualities of humility and restraint.

sturdy *adj.* 坚固的
alliance *n.* 联盟
entitle *v.* 使有权利

⑩ Our patchwork heritage is a strength, not a weakness. We are a nation of Christians and Muslims, Jews and Hindus, and non-believers. We are shaped by every language and culture, drawn from every end of this Earth; and because we have tasted the bitter swill of civil war and **segregation**, and emerged from that dark chapter stronger and more united, we cannot help but believe that the old hatreds shall someday pass; that the lines of tribe shall soon dissolve; that as the world grows smaller, our common humanity shall reveal itself; and that America must play its role in **ushering** in a new era of peace.

segregation *n.* 隔离

usher *v.* 引领

⑪ Our challenges may be new. The instruments with which we meet them may be new. But those values upon which our success depends—honesty and hard work, courage and fair play, tolerance and curiosity, loyalty and patriotism—these things are old. These things are true. They have been the quiet force of progress throughout our history.

⑫ At the moment when the outcome of our revolution was most in doubt, the father of our nation ordered these words to be read to the people: "Let it be told to the future world... that in the depth of winter, when nothing but hope and virtue could survive... that the city and the country, alarmed at one common danger, came forth to meet [it]."

⑬ America: In the face of our common dangers, in this winter of our hardship, let us remember these timeless words. With hope and virtue, let us brave once more the icy currents, and endure what storms may come. Let it be said by our children's children that when we were tested we refused to let this journey end, that we did not turn back nor did we **falter**; and with eyes fixed on the horizon and God's grace upon us, we carried forth that great gift of freedom and delivered it safely to future generations.

falter *v.* 犹豫，畏缩

⑭ Thank you. God bless you. And God bless the United States of America.

🎵 Extended Activities

Each of the following statements contains information given in one of the paragraphs in the passage. Identify the paragraph from which the information is derived and put the corresponding number in the space provided.

_____ 1) Our schools and colleges and universities will be transformed to meet the demands of a new age.

_____ 2) It was with the sturdy alliances and enduring convictions that earlier generations faced down fascism.

_____ 3) Americans are shaped by every language and culture, drawn from every end of this Earth.

_____ 4) It is well acknowledged that America is in the midst of a crisis.

_____ 5) Americans should remember these timeless words from the father of America in the face of dangers.

_____ 6) Americans must depend on old values such as honesty and hard work, courage and fair play, tolerance and curiosity, loyalty and patriotism to meet with new challenges.

_____ 7) The real concern of the public today is whether the government works rather than whether the government is too big or too small.

_____ 8) There are many serious real challenges in front of American people.

_____ 9) America is a friend of each nation, and every man, woman and child seeks a future of peace and dignity.

_____ 10) Obama thanked President Bush for his service as well as his generosity and cooperation.

2 Answer the following questions based on the understanding of the passage.

1) Why is America in the midst of a crisis, according to the speech?

2) What is the work to be done after President Obama takes office?

3) What do Americans care about concerning the government?

4) How do you understand the sentence "Our patchwork heritage is a strength, not a weakness" in Para. 10?

5) On what values do Americans depend to meet with new challenges?

3 Complete the following chart by filling in all major points in President Obama's inauguration speech. The first point has been given as an example.

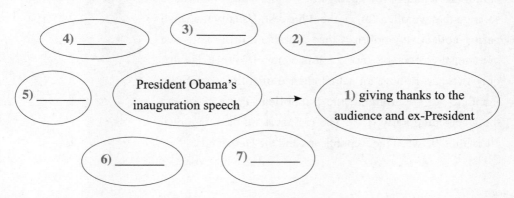

4 Work in pairs and retell the major content of President Obama's inauguration speech based on the information of Exercise 3. You may refer to the following words and expressions in your retelling.

values	transition	crisis	challenge	play its role
market	government	bless	grateful	timeless words

Exploring

Based on the two passages of this unit, think over the relationship between money and the presidential election in the U.S. Write an essay about it within 180 words. Your essay should include the following points:

- What role does money play in the American presidential election?
- Is the American presidential election money politics?

 # Mini-pedia

Two-party System

The American political system is a classical example of the two-party system. When we say that it has a two-party system in the United States, we do not mean that it has only two parties.

We call it a two-party system because it has two large parties and a number of small parties, and the large parties are so large that we often forget about the rest. Usually the small parties collectively poll less than 5 percent of the vote cast in national elections. However, it is common knowledge that only two parties have an actual chance of filling significant mandates in government: the Republican Party (RP) and the Democratic Party (DP). The U.S. system, then, is a dual alternation between the Republicans and the Democrats.

 # Reflection

Achievements	Yes	No
I have understood the function of campaign finance in the presidential election of the U.S.		
I am familiar with the language style of the presidential inauguration speech.		
I am aware of the difference in the political culture between China and the U.S.		
I have acquired useful words and expressions related to elections.		
I can share my opinion about the presidential election in the U.S. with international friends.		

UNIT 15

BREXIT

◇

GOALS

1 To know what Brexit is and the reason why Brexit happened;

2 To understand the impact of Brexit on Britain as well as the world;

3 To improve the ability of critical thinking;

4 To acquire some words and expressions about Brexit.

Warming-up

Answer the following questions:

1. How is the word "Brexit" formed?
2. Do you know why Brexit happened?
3. What influence will Brexit exert on Britain and the world?

Reading

Passage One Why Brexit Happened—and What To Do Next

❶ I am British.

❷ Never before has the phrase "I am British" **elicited** so much pity.

elicit *v.* 引出

❸ It came as an **immense** shock to me when I woke up on the morning of June 24 to discover that my country had voted to leave the European Union, my Prime Minister had resigned, and Scotland was considering a **referendum** that could bring to an end the very existence of the United Kingdom. So that was an immense shock for me, and it was an immense shock for many people, but it was also something that, over the following several days, created a complete political **meltdown** in my country. There were calls for a second referendum, almost as if, following a sports match, we could ask the opposition for a replay. Everybody was blaming everybody else. People blamed

immense *adj.* 巨大的

referendum *n.* 公民投票

meltdown *n.* 彻底垮台

the Prime Minister for calling the referendum in the first place. They blamed the leader of the opposition for not fighting it hard enough. The young accused the old. The educated blamed the less well-educated. That complete meltdown was made even worse by the most tragic element of it: levels of **xenophobia** and racist abuse in the streets of Britain at a level that I have never seen before in my lifetime. People are now talking about whether my country is becoming a Little England, or, as one of my colleagues put it, whether we're about to become a 1950s **nostalgia** theme park floating in the Atlantic Ocean.

xenophobia *n.* 对外国人的仇恨

nostalgia *n.* 怀旧

④　But my question is really, should we have the degree of shock that we've experienced since? Was it something that took place overnight? Or are there deeper structural factors that have led us to where we are today? So I want to take a step back and ask two very basic questions.

⑤　So first, what does Brexit represent? **Hindsight** is a wonderful thing. Brexit teaches us many things about our society and about societies around the world. It highlights in ways that we seem embarrassingly unaware of how divided our societies are. The vote split along lines of age, education, class and geography. Young people didn't turn out to vote in great numbers, but those that did want to remain. Older people really wanted to leave the European Union. Geographically, it was London and Scotland that most strongly committed to being part of the European Union, while in other parts of the country there was very strong **ambivalence**. Those divisions are things we really need to recognize and take seriously. But more profoundly, the vote teaches us something about the nature of politics today. Contemporary politics is no longer just about right and left. It's no longer just about tax and spend. It's about globalization. The fault line of contemporary politics is between those that embrace globalization and those that fear globalization.

hindsight *n.* 后见之明

ambivalence *n.* 矛盾情绪

⑥　If we look at why those who wanted to leave—we call them "Leavers", as opposed to "Remainers"—we see two factors in the opinion polls that really mattered. The first was immigration, and the second **sovereignty**, and these represent a desire for people to take back control of their own lives and the feeling that they are unrepresented by politicians. But those ideas are ones that signify fear and alienation. They represent a retreat back towards nationalism and borders in ways that many of us would reject. And the challenge that comes from that is we need to find a new way to narrate globalization to those people, to recognize that for those people who have not necessarily been to university, who haven't necessarily grown up with the Internet, that don't get opportunities to travel, they may be unpersuaded by the narrative that we find persuasive in our often liberal bubbles.

sovereignty n. 主权

❼ It means that we need to reach out more broadly and understand. In the Leave vote, a minority have peddled the politics of fear and hatred, creating lies and mistrust around, for instance, the idea that the vote on Europe could reduce the number of refugees and asylum-seekers coming to Europe, when the vote on leaving had nothing to do with immigration from outside the European Union. But for a significant majority of the Leave voters the concern was **disillusionment** with the political establishment. This was a protest vote for many, a sense that nobody represented them, that they couldn't find a political party that spoke for them, and so they rejected that political establishment.

disillusionment n. 幻灭

❽ This **replicates** around Europe and much of the liberal democratic world. We see it with the rise in popularity of Donald Trump in the United States, with the growing nationalism of Viktor Orbán in Hungary, with the increase in popularity of Marine Le Pen in France. The specter of Brexit is in all of our societies.

replicate v. 复制

❾ So the question I think we need to ask is my second question, which is how should we **collectively** respond? For all of us who care about creating liberal, open, tolerant societies, we urgently need a new vision, a vision of a more tolerant, inclusive globalization, one that brings people with us rather than leaving them behind.

collectively adv. 共同地

⑩　In 2002, the former Secretary-General of the United Nations, Kofi Annan, gave a speech at Yale University, and that speech was on the topic of inclusive globalization. That was the speech in which he coined that term. And he said, and I paraphrase, "The glass house of globalization has to be open to all if it is to remain secure. **Bigotry** and ignorance are the ugly face of **exclusionary** and **antagonistic** globalization."

bigotry *n.* 偏执
exclusionary *adj.* 排他的
antagonistic *adj.* 敌对的

⑪　The question is, how can we achieve that goal? How can we balance on the one hand addressing fear and alienation while on the other hand refusing vehemently to give in to xenophobia and nationalism? Our transformation has to be about both ideas and about material change, and I want to give you four ideas as a starting point.

⑫　The first relates to the idea of civic education. What stands out from Brexit is the gap between public perception and **empirical** reality. It's been suggested that we've moved to a post-factual society, where evidence and truth no longer matter, and lies have equal status to the clarity of evidence. How can we rebuild respect for truth and evidence into our liberal democracies? It has to begin with education, but it has to start with the recognition that there are huge gaps. It has to be about lifelong civic participation and public engagement that we all encourage as societies.

empirical *adj.* 经验主义的

⑬　The second thing that I think is an opportunity is the idea to encourage more interaction across diverse communities.

⑭　One of the things that stands out for me very strikingly, looking at immigration attitudes in the United Kingdom, is that ironically, the regions of my country that are the most tolerant of immigrants have the highest numbers of immigrants. So for instance, London and the Southeast have the highest numbers of immigrants, and they are also by far the most tolerant areas. It's those areas of the country that have the lowest levels of immigration that actually are the most exclusionary and intolerant towards migrants.

⑮   So we need to encourage exchange programs. We need to ensure that older generations who maybe can't travel get access to the Internet. We need to encourage, even on a local and national level, more movement, more participation, more interaction with people who we don't know and whose views we might not necessarily agree with.

⑯   The third thing that I think is crucial, though, and this is really fundamental, is we have to ensure that everybody shares in the benefits of globalization. This illustration from the *Financial Times* post-Brexit is really striking. It shows tragically that those people who voted to leave the European Union were those who actually benefited the most materially from trade with the European Union. But the problem is that those people in those areas didn't perceive themselves to be **beneficiaries**. They didn't believe that they were actually getting access to material benefits of increased trade and increased mobility around the world.

beneficiary *n.* 受惠者

⑰   The fourth and final idea I want to put forward is an idea that we need more responsible politics. There's very little social science evidence that compares attitudes on globalization. But from the surveys that do exist, what we can see is there's huge variation across different countries and time periods in those countries for attitudes and tolerance of questions like migration and mobility on the one hand and free trade on the other. But one **hypothesis** that I think emerges from a **cursory** look at that data is the idea that **polarized** societies are far less tolerant of globalization. It's the societies like Sweden in the past, like Canada today, where there is a centrist politics, where right and left work together, that we encourage supportive attitudes towards globalization. And what we see around the world today is a tragic polarization, a failure to have dialogue between the extremes in politics, and a gap in terms of that liberal center ground that can encourage communication and a shared understanding. We might not achieve that today, but at the very least we have to call upon our politicians and our media to drop a language of fear and be far more tolerant of one another.

hypothesis *n.* 假设
cursory *adj.* 粗略的
polarized *adj.* 极化的

I am still British. I am still European. I am still a global citizen. For those of us who believe that our identities are not mutually exclusive, we have to all work together to ensure that globalization takes everyone with us and doesn't leave people behind. Only then will we truly **reconcile** democracy and globalization.

reconcile *v.* 使一致；使和解

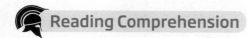

Reading Comprehension

Answer the following questions based on the understanding of the passage.

1) What did the speaker find when he woke up on the morning of June 24th, 2016?
2) What happened in the following several days after June 24th, 2016?
3) Can you explain in detail how the vote split along lines of age, education, class and geography?
4) How should we collectively respond according to the speaker?
5) What ideas did the speaker put forward as for how to achieve inclusive globalization?

Decide whether the following statements are true or false. Write T for true and F for false.

_____ 1) There were calls for a second referendum after the result of the referendum came out.

_____ 2) Most people in London and Scotland wanted to leave the European Union.

_____ 3) It was Barack Obama who coined the term "inclusive globalization".

_____ 4) According to the speaker, the regions of the U.K. that are the most tolerant of immigrants have the highest numbers of immigrants.

_____ 5) According to the speaker, those people who voted to leave the European Union were those who didn't benefit the most materially from trade with the European Union.

Fill in the following table with the information from the passage.

Parts	Paras.	Main Ideas
Part I Phenomenon	1–1) _____	There was a complete 2) _____ in the U.K. after the result of the referendum was issued on June 24th, 2016.

Parts	Paras.	Main Ideas
Part II Reasons	3) _____ – 4) _____	The speaker analyzed why Brexit happened. There are two factors. The first was 5) _____, and the second 6) _____.
Part III Solutions	7) _____ – 18	The speaker put forward 8) _____ ideas to achieve 9) _____.

Language in Use

Complete the table with the correct form of the words given. Then complete the sentences with the correct form of the words in the table.

Nouns	Verbs	Adjectives
globalization		
		persuasive
	replicate	
		collective
alienation		
	polarize	
		inclusive
		exclusive
perception		
mobility		

1) He has _____ his error after having talked with his father.

2) And what is true of individuals is also true for _____ entities, like states and cities.

3) It's interesting, and you can see that's a very _____ argument, but you can also see how that could be abused.

4) The country as a whole was thoroughly _____ into Leavers and Remainers.

5) There is a big budget science-fiction movie about humans on a(an) _____ planet.

6) And then they can download the PDF file to _____ them at home.

7) If two things are mutually _____, they are separate and very different from each other, so that it is impossible for them to exist or happen together.

8) In a _____ society, people move easily from one job, home, or social class to another.

9) _____ warming is becoming a more and more serious issue.

10) And it's an all-_____ ticket. That's a really good thing to do.

⑤ Translate the following paragraph into Chinese.

It means that we need to reach out more broadly and understand. In the Leave vote, a minority have peddled the politics of fear and hatred, creating lies and mistrust around, for instance, the idea that the vote on Europe could reduce the number of refugees and asylum-seekers coming to Europe, when the vote on leaving had nothing to do with immigration from outside the European Union. But for a significant majority of the Leave voters the concern was disillusionment with the political establishment. This was a protest vote for many, a sense that nobody represented them, that they couldn't find a political party that spoke for them, and so they rejected that political establishment.

Oral Practice

⑥ Read the passage again and discuss with your partner about what happened in the U.K. after the vote for Brexit and what measures people can take to reduce the negative impact of Brexit by using the following expressions.

| referendum | shock | meltdown | blame | globalization |
| immigrant | abuse | inclusive | diverse | civic education |

Passage Two Brexit

What does Brexit mean?

① Brexit is a word that has become used as a shorthand way of saying the U.K. is leaving the EU—merging the words Britain and exit to get Brexit, in the same way as a possible Greek exit from the euro.

Why is Britain leaving the European Union?

❷　A referendum—a vote in which everyone (or nearly everyone) of voting age can take part—was held on Thursday, June 23, 2016, to decide whether the U.K. should leave or remain in the European Union. Leave won by 51.9% to 48.1%. The referendum **turnout** was 71.8%, with more than 30 million people voting.

turnout *n.* 结果

What was the breakdown across the U.K.?

❸　England voted for Brexit, by 53.4% to 46.6%. Wales also voted for Brexit, with Leave getting 52.5% of the vote and Remain 47.5%. Scotland and Northern Ireland both backed staying in the EU. Scotland backed Remain by 62% to 38%, while 55.8% in Northern Ireland voted Remain and 44.2% Leave.

What changed in government after the referendum?

❹　Britain got a new Prime Minister—Theresa May. The former home secretary took over from David Cameron, who announced he was resigning on the day he lost the referendum. Like Mr. Cameron, Mrs. May was against Britain leaving the EU but she played only a very **low-key** role in the campaign and was never seen as much of an enthusiast for the EU. She became PM without facing a full Conservative leadership contest after her key rivals from what had been the Leave side pulled out.

low-key *adj.* 低调的

Why has she called a general election?

❺　Theresa May became prime minister after David Cameron resigned, so she has not won her own election. She ruled out calling a **snap** election when she moved into Downing Street, saying the country needed a period of stability after the **upheaval** of the Brexit vote. She said she was happy to wait until the next scheduled election in 2020.

snap *adj.* 突然的
upheaval *n.* 巨变

❻　But she surprised everyone after the Easter Bank Holiday by announcing that she had changed her mind with an election being called for Thursday, June 8, 2017.

❼ The reason she gave was that she needed to strengthen her hand in Brexit negotiations with European leaders. She feared Labour, the SNP and other opposition parties—and members of the House of Lords—would try to block and frustrate her strategy, making the country look divided to other EU leaders and making her government look weak.

❽ Mrs. May inherited a tiny Commons majority from David Cameron, meaning that it only takes a few Conservative MPs to side with the opposition to vote down the government's plans. The Conservatives began the election campaign with a big lead over Labour in the opinion polls. Recent polls have suggested the gap has closed, but still put the Conservatives in front.

What about the economy, so far?

❾ David Cameron, his **Chancellor** George Osborne and many other senior figures who wanted to stay in the EU predicted an immediate economic crisis if the U.K. voted to leave. House prices would fall, there would be a **recession** with a big rise in unemployment—and an emergency budget would be needed to bring in the large cuts in spending that would be needed.

chancellor *n.* 大使

recession *n.* 衰退

❿ The pound did **slump** the day after the referendum—and remains around 15% lower against the dollar and 10% down against the euro—but the predictions of immediate doom have not proved accurate with the U.K. economy estimated to have grown 1.8% in 2016, second only to Germany's 1.9% among the world's G7 leading industrialised nations.

slump *v.* 暴跌

⓫ **Inflation** has risen—to 2.6% in April—its highest rate for three and a half years, but unemployment has continued to fall, to stand at an 11 year low of 4.8%. Annual house price increases have fallen from 9.4% in June but were still at an inflation-busting 4.1% in March, according to official **ONS** figures.

inflation *n.* 通货膨胀

ONS 国家统计局

What is Article 50?

⑫ Article 50 is a plan for any country that wishes to exit the EU. It was created as part of the Treaty of Lisbon—an agreement signed up by all EU states which became law in 2009. Before that treaty, there was no formal mechanism for a country to leave the EU.

⑬ It's pretty short—just five paragraphs—which spell out that any EU member state may decide to quit the EU, that it must notify the European Council and negotiate its withdrawal with the EU, that there are two years to reach an agreement—unless everyone agrees to extend it—and that the exiting state cannot take part in EU internal discussions about its departure.

What date will the U.K. leave the EU?

⑭ For the U.K. to leave the EU it had to **invoke** Article 50 of the Lisbon Treaty which gives the two sides two years to agree to the terms of the split. Theresa May triggered this process on March 29, meaning the U.K. is scheduled to leave on Friday, March 29, 2019. It can be extended if all 28 EU members agree.

invoke v. 启动

How long will it take for Britain to leave the EU?

⑮ Once Article 50 is triggered, the U.K. has two years to negotiate its withdrawal. But no one really knows how the Brexit process will work—Article 50 was only created in late 2009 and it has never been used. Former Foreign Secretary Philip Hammond, who was appointed chancellor by Theresa May, wanted Britain to remain in the EU during the referendum campaign and suggested it could take up to six years for the U.K. to complete exit negotiations. The terms of Britain's exit will have to be agreed by 27 national parliaments, a process which could take some years, he has argued.

⑯ EU law still stands in the U.K. until it ceases being a member. The U.K. will continue to abide by EU treaties and laws, but not take part in any decision-making.

Why will Brexit take so long?

17 Unpicking 43 years of treaties and agreements covering thousands of different subjects was never going to be a straightforward task. It is further complicated by the fact that it has never been done before and negotiators will, to some extent, be making it up as they go along. The post-Brexit trade deal is likely to be the most complex part of the negotiation because it needs the **unanimous** approval of more than 30 national and regional parliaments across Europe, some of whom may want to hold referendums.

unanimous *adj.* 全体一致的

What do "soft" and "hard" Brexit mean?

18 These terms have increasingly been used as debate focused on the terms of the U.K.'s departure from the EU. There is no strict definition of either, but they are used to refer to the closeness of the U.K.'s relationship with the EU post-Brexit.

19 So at one extreme, "hard" Brexit could involve the U.K. refusing to compromise on issues like the free movement of people even if meant leaving the single market. At the other end of the scale, a "soft" Brexit might follow a similar path to Norway, which is a member of the single market and has to accept the free movement of people as a result of that.

 ## Extended Activities

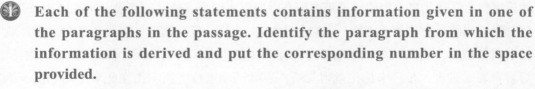 **Each of the following statements contains information given in one of the paragraphs in the passage. Identify the paragraph from which the information is derived and put the corresponding number in the space provided.**

    _____ 1) "Soft" and "hard" Brexit are used to refer to the closeness of the U.K.'s relationship with the EU post-Brexit.

    _____ 2) Theresa May triggered this process on March 29, meaning the U.K. is scheduled to leave on Friday, March 29, 2019.

_____ 3) The post-Brexit trade deal needs the unanimous approval of more than 30 national and regional parliaments across Europe, some of whom may want to hold referendums.

_____ 4) Theresa May ruled out calling a snap election when she moved into Downing Street.

_____ 5) However, unemployment has continued to fall after the referendum in the U.K.

_____ 6) Article 50 has never been used after being created in late 2009.

_____ 7) Brexit is a word that has become used as a shorthand way of saying the U.K. is leaving the EU.

_____ 8) The pound dropped sharply on the day after the referendum.

_____ 9) Recent polls have shown that the Conservative party still takes a minor lead over the Labour party.

_____ 10) Article 50 is pretty short—just five paragraphs—which spell out that any EU member state may decide to quit the EU, that it must notify the European Council and negotiate its withdrawal with the EU.

Answer the following questions based on the understanding of the passage.

1) What is Brexit and what was the result of the referendum on June 23rd, 2016?

2) Why has Theresa May called a general election?

3) What impact does the referendum result impose on the British economy?

4) What is Article 50?

5) Why is there a long way to go for Britain to break up with the EU completely?

Translate the following paragraph into English.

英国民众于 6 月 23 日举行了全国公投，就是否继续留在欧盟做出决定。卡梅伦说，"这次公投将会决定英国在以后几十年里、也有可能是一生的命运"，并补充说："这是一个比任何政治家和政府更重要的决定"。卡梅伦在周一的时候发表了这篇演讲，评论家们将其称为自卡梅伦劝说英国留在欧盟以来最令人感动的演讲。调查显示，"保留"派给出的最有力的原因之一是在过去的 70 年里，欧盟国家一直处于和平之中。就在卡梅伦结束演讲后不久，包括部分保守党成员（卡梅伦本身属于保守党）在内的反对者发表了谴责，批评卡梅伦危言耸听。退欧活动家指责唐宁街在此事上的恐慌，尽管此前奥巴马和其他一些领导人曾介入，希望英国留在欧盟。

Exploring

Debating: Should Britain leave the European Union or not?

Step 1 The whole class is divided into two groups, and one group is in the leaving campaign while the other is in the remaining campaign.

Step 2 Work out points and supporting details.

Step 3 One member of each group presents the group's points and supporting details within 4 minutes.

Step 4 Free debating.

Step 5 One member of each group summarizes the points.

 # Mini-pedia

Top 10 Collins Words of the Year 2016*

Brexit has been named Collins Word of the Year 2016 thanks to a dramatic increase in usage. Here's the words that made the top 10 list.

Brexit

The withdrawal of the United Kingdom from the European Union

Hygge

A concept, originating in Denmark, of creating cosy and convivial atmospheres that promote wellbeing

Mic drop

A theatrical gesture in which a person drops (or imitates the action of dropping) a hand-held microphone to the ground as the finale to a speech or performance

Trumpism

(1) the policies advocated by the U.S. politician Donald Trump, especially those involving a rejection of the current

political establishment and the vigorous pursuit of American national interests (2) a controversial or outrageous statement attributed to Donald Trump

Throw shade

To make a public show of contempt for someone or something, often in a subtle or non-verbal manner

Sharenting

The habitual use of social media to share news, images, etc. of one's children

Snowflake generation

The young adults of the 2010s, viewed as being less resilient and more prone to taking offence than previous generations

Dude food

Junk food such as hot dogs, burgers, etc. considered particularly appealing to men

Uberisation

The adoption of a business model in which services are offered on demand through direct contact between a customer and supplier, usually via mobile technology

JOMO

Joy of missing out: pleasure gained from enjoying one's current activities without worrying that other people are having more fun

Posted by Collins Language Thursday November 03, 2016

 # Reflection

Achievements	Yes	No
I know what Brexit is and the reason why Brexit happened.		
I have understood the impact of Brexit on Britain as well as the world.		
My ability of critical thinking is improved.		
I have acquired some words and expressions about Brexit.		